What People Are Saying...

God provided me with an incredible role model and mentor in Paul Sebastian, a dear friend since the early '60s when he gave me a mimeograph machine for printing Gospel literature. He tremendously encouraged Donna and me throughout the years we served in China, and he is one of our most trusted prayer warriors. You too will be blessed by reading Son of a Blacksmith, *an amazing account of God's faithfulness and Paul's sterling character.*

> John Bechtel
> Regional Director Asia
> Ravi Zachariah International Ministries

This book is an inspiring, honest and unvarnished account of Paul's childhood to this present time – a story that reaches out to all of us. Over the past forty years I have watched Paul model perseverance, following God faithfully in every aspect of life. This memorable story is a lifelong study of what commitment to God looks like.

> Rev. Dr. Grover G. DeVault
> Chaplain (Lieutenant Colonel) USA Ret.

One of the things I personally enjoyed about Paul's book is the plethora of pictures, especially the before and after comparisons. The story of the Trust Building intrigued me; how God brought together details over the years and across Lancaster County. I didn't immediately see the significance of the stained-glass window on the cover until I read about Paul's LBC window. Son of a Blacksmith *is the perfect book to be included in our renovated section of the bookstore geared toward college visitors.*

> Mark Blest
> Director of Retail Services and *Bookends* Manager
> Lancaster Bible College

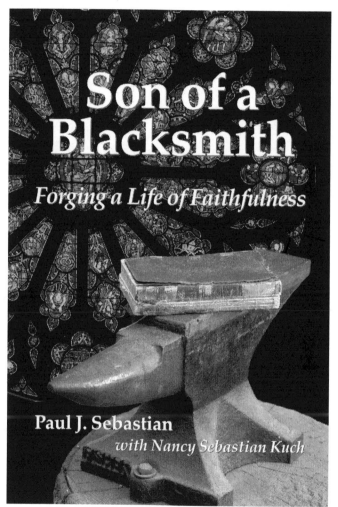

Son of a Blacksmith

Forging a Life of Faithfulness

Paul J. Sebastian

with Nancy Sebastian Kuch

COVER
My father, James E. Sebastian, created the iron framework supporting Lawrence
Saint's stained-glass in the North Rose Window of the National Cathedral in Washington
D.C. (Public Domain)
Also pictured is Dad's actual anvil and Mom's well-worn Bible from which she
frequently read to me. (Photo by Keith Baum)

Dedications

To dearest Jeanne – Jean is my wife, friend and the love of my life,
Always faithful, wise, insightful and godly.
All my love,
— Paul

To my husband Larry,
Thank you for your astounding skills in wordsmithing, editing and design,
and for your love, patience and exquisite partnership.
— Nancy

All profit from this book will go to Lancaster Bible College.
Thank you for investing in the lives of
Christian students training to serve the Lord.

If you wish to further support LBC students, please contact:
Lancaster Bible College
901 Eden Road, Lancaster, PA 17601
www.lbc.edu

Contents

More content available at sonofablacksmith.com

Foreword

To sum up this remarkable man in a word it would be *faithful*. When Paul tells me he prays for me, he means it. When he says every day, he means it.

I first met Paul J. Sebastian through Lancaster Bible College when I became a trustee. At that time this 1952 alumnus had already served 14 years on the board and would go on to serve at least 27 more. I could never have imagined how Paul would influence my life and presidency as a chief encourager and prayer warrior.

Over the years, Paul has performed many roles at LBC — teacher, architect, campus development engineer — and today he continues to share wisdom and insights as a member of our Board of Trustees, Building Committee, and Corporation. He has also been a member of Calvary Church since 1961. And God still uses this 93-year-old in His plan as Paul designs, invents and consults throughout his "retirement."

In this chronicle, you will read about Paul's life experiences. From a family of humble means and reliance upon God, he recalls the Great Depression, World War II, and adventures relating to college, business, photography, food and family.

After reading this account of Paul's life, I believe these three words express what matters most to him: *family, focus and faith.*

There is perhaps one more noun I would use as an umbrella descriptor of Paul J. Sebastian, assuredly the most important word of all: *friend.*

Peter W. Teague, Ed.D.
President, Lancaster Bible College

Introductory Thoughts and Thanks

B lacksmiths—like my dad—forge iron into useful instruments and beauti-ful art. As I step back and view the past 90 years, I see how God has faithfully worked my life into something usable and beautiful...and I am amazed. I can say with all confidence that God is creative, sovereign and trust-worthy. (*See page 1 for more on blacksmithing.*)

It is my hope and goal in writing this book to help you see what a relationship with my God and Savior looks like. Your story may be very different, but God can be just as faithful, loving and true to you. If He can do exceedingly abundantly above all that I've ever asked or thought according to His power at work within me, He can do the same for you.

Because biographical reciting of names, dates and details often bores readers—even close family—I have chosen something of a memoir style of writing, using sensory impressions and personal interpretation of events. Although the book is divided into chronological sections of my life, I occasionally jump around to make connections or draw conclusions. Appendix A provides a timeline of my crucial life events.

If you want to go even further back in time, you could read the history of my family, prior to my birth, in Appendix B. We chose not to make it Chapter 1 because this information was told to me rather than experienced, therefore told with a different voice and feel than the rest of the book.

Appendix C includes old letters my daughter Nancy found in our search for photographs and memorabilia for the book. She chose only a few and edited them for ease of reading and interest.

Nancy was first to identify an interesting subtheme in my stories and dub me a "foodie." Thus we included Appendix D, favorite recipes I have enjoyed throughout my life (and which I delighted in sampling as we prepared each recipe for inclusion in the book). We think you, too, may add them to your family favorites.

The use of additional names and the relating of situations in this book are my truth to the best of my knowledge and remembrance. A few of my memories include painful circumstances or difficult relationships. I have thoughtfully considered and prayed over what God wanted me to include in order that you might glean encouragement from the moments and lessons shared.

My greatest hope is that you who read this book will be challenged to a new or deeper walk with Jesus Christ and meet me in Heaven one day where we can talk of how God used *your* life for His glory.

I thank Nancy for her love and encouragement, as well as tireless hours of editing and design. She rearranged and made my words flow like honey. I also thank her husband, Larry, for his expert editing and layout skills. He was truly qualified for this work with his education as a seminary graduate and experience as a Wycliffe missionary in Ghana, West Africa where he wrote primers and language materials and translated the entire book of Mark.

I dedicate this book to my loving wife, Jean, my closest friend and helpmate every step of the way. I am grateful to my parents for my upbringing — my mother who nurtured me and my loving dad, a wise father and creative blacksmith from whom I gained so many attributes, traits and skills. I also thank all those who have encouraged me to tell these stories, chief of which was Joel DeHart, son of my best friend Don. And thank *you* for reading.

Blacksmithing

The sights, sounds and smells of my dad's blacksmith shop created an intriguing environment for a formative boy growing up on the outskirts of Philadelphia amidst the Great Depression. To clarify, Dad was a gifted craftsman of wrought iron, as opposed to a farrier, whose primary job was to shoe horses.

What I witnessed as Dad used fire and force to craft a slab of metal into an object of purpose and beauty is exactly what God has been doing with my life over these past many years. Thus I have entitled my story *Son of a Blacksmith: Forging a Life of Faithfulness.*

Blacksmithing is both a science and an art. A successful blacksmith thoroughly understands the use of heat, carefully monitoring the metal in the depths of the fire. But he must also possess an artist's eye for detail, symmetry and beauty.

My dad used the finest iron in the world, called Swedish wrought iron. It contained a portion of nickel alloy that resisted oxidation (rusting) when exposed to the elements. Today, wrought iron is no longer produced anywhere in the world, necessitating salvaging from old gates, fences and the like. Often mild steel is used as a substitute. The blacksmith derives his title from the fact that both iron and steel are considered black metals.

Today, as in Dad's time, the knowledge and practice of smithing is passed down, person to person, hammer in hand. I salute the master blacksmith who taught my dad the trade. Although I experienced the hot and messy work in my adolescence as I helped Dad, I gladly passed up blacksmithing for the life of a draftsman, also a trade based on science and art.

Recalling memories and organizing them into this book has helped me see God's workmanship in my life. You will read about my times in the fire as well as when He has had to pound sense into me! How thankful I am for God's faithfulness, protection and love as He continues to craft the heart of this old man. I'm still a work in progress.

Chapter 1

Early Years and Family

My eyes, about even with Grandma Coeyman's apron pockets, didn't miss a thing. In fact, I frequently observed her handkerchief fly from pocket to mouth as she coughed. Just a little cough. Mother had taught me that covering your mouth when you coughed or sneezed showed good manners, so I was dutifully impressed.

Carefully scrutinizing Grandma, however, it dawned on me one day that with each cough she circumspectly transported a peppermint candy from her pocket to her lips. I wanted one too, of course, but satisfied myself with knowing her little secret. After all, children of that time were "seen and not heard," so it would have been totally unacceptable to mention anything about those moving peppermints.

Grandma, my mom's step-mother, had no children of her own. She wasn't exactly mean, but she sure was grumpy during her visits several times each year. Piled high on her head in a bun, her yellowish-gray hair always looked kind of dirty. Her wrinkled common-looking face seldom held a smile. But I liked the way she smelled…a little minty.

I knew very little about Grandfather Coeyman, because he passed away in the first few years of my life (the late 1920s). I am thankful for at least one very early recollection of him. I can picture him standing with my grandmother looking in at me from the doorway of my bedroom. I vaguely remember pulling myself upright using the rungs of my crib. Probably in a teething stage, I recall soothing my gums on the cold top rail of the iron crib that

Harry and Ellen Coyeman, my maternal grandparents, pose with me in one of my earliest pictures, dated Summer 1926.

was covered with chipped white paint. My grandparents waved at me, smiling, as I continued to suck on the cool metal.

Grandma eventually moved to an old folks' home. The facility was not a nice place and always smelled like an outhouse. Sometimes the crabby matron would not let us see Grandma, telling us she was napping. Mom always took along a homemade cake and rice pudding. The matron would take our goodies and assure us Grandma would get them when she awoke. I can still hear Mom saying on the way home, "I'll just bet that matron eats our desserts herself and they never make it to Grandma."

Grandmother Bastian, Aunt Jo and Riverton

Sadly, I remember far less pleasant experiences with Grandma Bastian (our Sebastian relatives adopted a shortened version of the name for a time). She

Prim and proper Caroline Bastian was my paternal grandmother.

stood tall, regal and stern. Clean, neat and carefully dressed, she always wore a thick velvet ribbon around her neck and secured it at the base of her throat with a cameo, an oval pin with a raised profile. As I got older and became more observant, I realized she had a neck wattle, extra folds of skin that came with age. This problem apparently embarrassed her since she took such pains to cover it.

One of the things I liked least about Grandma was her penchant to speak her mind. She once told my mother she had teeth like a horse. Mom, who had nice large teeth that I thought fit her features, is almost always pictured smiling with her mouth closed. But I remember a woman who laughed frequently, loud and long—with her mouth open. My mother was full of joy, as opposed to Grandma who was not.

Residing in Williamsport, Pennsylvania, Grandma lived with her only daughter, Josephine. But she spent one month each winter with son Walter's family and one month with us.

Grandma seemed to enjoy visiting my house at 15 Cherry Street in Willow Grove, Pennsylvania, a northern suburb of Philadelphia. In the late '20s and early '30s, my town was a major transportation hub with big highways going in every direction, an abundance of trolleys and busses, and the train station. Willow Grove also boasted a first-class amusement park with band concerts by the likes of John Philip Sousa and Arthur Pryor. And of course, we were right outside the bustling metropolitan and historic city of Philadelphia.

When she came to visit, Grandma spent considerable time rocking on our front porch, reading book after book. Besides reading, she enjoyed traveling and shopping. Many times, she took a day trip to John Wannamaker's department store in Philadelphia, most always forgetting to bring me a promised present. I wondered why she bothered to tell me she would bring me something if she

Aunt Josephine's summer home boasted spacious gardens
along the Susquehanna River in Williamsport.

never intended to do so.

Each summer we spent a week visiting Grandma and Aunt Jo at Riverton, my aunt's beautiful summer residence along the Susquehanna River near Williamsport. Although not as handsome as my mom, Aunt Jo was very jolly, always smiling and genuine. She didn't put on airs. Perhaps she could be like that because she was very wealthy and was not trying to be someone she was not. Aunt Jo was very kind and generous to my sister Josie and me. Today I might describe Aunt Jo as having a Type A personality. Always active, she was constantly doing something for us or around her house.

Aunt Jo's husband, Nathaniel Canfield, had become very wealthy through the lumber industry but passed away before I first met Aunt Josephine. Two live-in black maids attended to Aunt Jo's every need. They traveled with her to both of her lovely homes: a house in the city of Williamsport and her summer estate on the river. Riverton boasted extensive flower gardens, Jo's pride and joy. I remember Aunt Jo pointing out a prize tulip to my dad, saying she sent to Holland for it at a cost of $17 per bulb (this was Dad's approximate monthly income at that time, during the Great Depression).

Our trips to visit Grandma and Aunt Jo usually took a full day (now it takes but a few hours to go those 90 miles on today's highways). We didn't count the miles as much as the number of flat tires it took to get there and back—usually two or three flats each way in our

One summer my sister Josie visited Aunt Jo in Williamsport and attended a girls' camp for a week. She shocked my mother when she returned with a new, short "bobbed" hair style; Aunt Jo said, "She needed to look like the other girls." My mother grieved the loss of Josie's long curls, pictured here.

old Apperson touring car. A big bang was followed by wobbling to a stop on the rim. Dad jacked up the car, examined the tire's inner tube for the split, and repaired it with rubber patch and cement. If the hole in the inner tube was bad enough, he replaced it with one of the three or four he had tied on the back of the car. Then he would pump up the tire and off we'd go...until the next flat.

To hold our luggage, a pantograph carrier was attached to the running board (step) by the driver's door; so we got in and out on the passenger side of the car. We traditionally made a stop in Hershey and bought two boxes of solid chocolate Hershey bonbons, one for Aunt Jo and one for us.

Multiple times throughout each trip, Dad had to pull over to a railroad station and Mom and my sister Josie would get out and go inside. When I asked him about it, he just said, "They have weak kidneys." I wondered about that for a while until I figured it out.

If we got lucky, we would find a picnic table alongside the side of the road around lunch time. Otherwise we would eat Mom's packed lunch in the car. Since this was a vacation, sandwiches were made with ham instead of jelly. We had cake, too, because desserts were big back then. Dad always carried two big thermos bottles that each had several cups under the lid. Every time we stopped, he poured water for each of us.

One time, Mom couldn't find the bananas she had packed. Later we realized she had sat on them almost from the beginning of the trip, and we all had a good laugh.

Once I remember standing up in the back seat behind mother, pointing to a road sign, and saying, "Look. 'Chicken Dinner: All You Can Eat for $1!' Can we stop?"

Mother responded in a familiar commanding tone, "Paul, no one can eat that much—not a dollar's worth. Sit down."

I sat down.

Visiting Aunt Jo and Grandma one summer, we attended the Sunday service at Grandma's church. At the conclusion, Mother told me to be on my very best behavior because Grandma was taking us to the YMCA for dinner. I cannot come close to describing my excitement, since my family could not afford to eat in restaurants. The elegant, multi-story YMCA building boasted a fancy dining room with crystal chandeliers, tables covered with snowy white cloths, and scrumptious food. The whole dining-out experience created quite a memory for this impressionable little boy.

A food enthusiast, I enjoyed visiting my relatives in part because almost all of them were excellent cooks and bakers. This was quite true at Aunt Jo's estate. I most fondly remember her huge sugar cookies with a plump raisin snuggled in the center of each one, a treat for completing the various jobs she assigned to me at our arrival each visit. I always looked forward to helping out at Aunt Jo's...and, of course, I greatly anticipated her cookies.

At five or six, I recall Grandma Bastian sternly and constantly correcting me, calling me "Baby." Once in a great while, she would read to me. One particular time I remember her reading a book about farm animals reproducing their young. I stopped her to ask how that happens, and she assured me I would learn about it as I got older. Indeed, a few years later my cousin George took me to Just-a-Farm in Bucks County where I witnessed the birth of a calf. I still remember that beautiful farm with its acres and acres of green pastures.

During Grandma Bastian's visits, she occupied the front room on the third floor of our Cherry Street home. After she passed away, I was given that room for my standard gauge Lionel trains. I had an enviable collection of trains in a display I kept up year-round. It was my winter "sport" when the weather wouldn't allow me to play baseball. Dad made sure Santa never forgot me at Christmas; each year I found one or two items I had circled in the Lionel Catalog under the Christmas tree. I kept my display going for several years before I had to give up the room to a boarder, my cousin Richard.

Lionel standard gauge trains were a year-round hobby for me. I enjoyed designing various track layouts even more than running the trains.

Cousin Richard and Flying

I was only three when Charles Lindbergh made his famous 1927 Transatlantic Flight from New York to Paris. Although I cannot remember the event itself, I heard talk of it for many years following. Boy, I loved the thought of flying! And as far back as I can remember I made little planes out anything I could find. My balsa wood projects powered by rubber bands flew the best. And I can easily remember each airplane that flew over Willow Grove.

Throughout the '20s and '30s, the early years of aviation, airplanes fascinated almost everyone. People were so curious to see planes in flight, they would run out of their homes, look up and point, and call out to others. A biplane (having two wings, one over the other) was the usual sight, a noisy thing that struggled through the air as many spectators on the ground, including me, wondered what kept it up there.

During the annual Memorial Day Parade, planes flew over the town and dropped rosebuds on the parade route in honor of the fallen servicemen of World War I. During the years I marched in the high school band, I was disappointed that we were not allowed to break ranks to gather rosebuds.

Lucky for me, we had a pilot in the family. Richard S. Balwin was the son of my great aunt Sarah Speyerer who lived in Rochester (Beaver County, PA). She beautifully hand-painted china, and some of her remarkable platters, plates, cups and saucers still grace our home today. Her husband was a judge in the city. Richard was well-educated, earning degrees from Massachusetts Institute of Technology (MIT) in mechanical, marine and aeronautical engineering.

One day during my preteens, Richard stopped for a short visit at our home on his way to the Philadelphia Navy Yard to accept a job as a designer in their engineering department. Mother invited him to supper and encouraged him to stay with us until he found a permanent residence. Instead of a few weeks, this bachelor ended up living in our home for the next 20 years (he, too, considered my mother an outstanding cook).

Dick, as I called him, flew single-engine planes as a hobby. My best buddy Jimmy Cunningham and I made small parachutes out of cloth and string and attached them to stones. Dick flew over our house and dropped our inventions out his window. Jimmy and I had great fun watching for him and retrieving the tiny fliers from neighboring yards.

I was about fourteen when Dick finally convinced Mom and Dad of the safety of flight. To my ecstasy, they gave me permission to be his passenger. Many Saturdays he took me along for a ride, flying out of a variety of private Philadelphia airports. He kept a log of his flying time in which he recorded thousands of hours in the cockpits of little single-engine propeller-driven planes. I learned firsthand many things about flying small airplanes. On very rare occasions, he let me fly after we took off or before we landed. Because of those moments in the cockpit, I decided I wanted to be a fighter pilot someday.

In the fall of each year Richard took me along on various escapades. We visited farm shows to see the animals, went to horse races, and ate hot dogs. I loved hunting groundhogs with his 220 Swift Model 70 Winchester rifle. Great fun!

Reflections on Mom

My mom was surely a gifted person, especially in knowing how to be my mother. Prior to my birth and on the heels of World War I, an influenza epidemic swept the world, killing my older brother James (age 4) and leaving my sister Josie (age 6) very weak. Devastated, Mom and Dad begged God for another boy. God answered in less than a year. Realizing she was pregnant, Mom chose birth by caesarean section—she wasn't going to take what she

Years later (after I married), Richard took Jean and me on short flights in his Taylor (now Piper) Cub. When Dick manned the controls, I often seized the opportunity to practice taking good aerial pictures.

thought were chances with my life after losing a child.

Mom watched over me and protected me. She couldn't do enough for me. And she harbored great expectations for me. She would say, "God's watching over you. Don't disappoint Him," as she instructed me to be well-behaved.

Mom was an exceptionally good cook, provider and encourager. She seemed to be able to make something out of almost anything, or nothing at all. During the Great Depression, when jobs were super scarce and people had little if any money, she wore a new hat to church every Sunday. The ladies would twitter about her hat after the service, and she enjoyed telling them how she remade last week's hat. That same creativity enabled us to enjoy delicious meals every day during hard times, meals that filled

This studio portrait shows my mother about the time she married Dad.

our home with appetizing aromas and our bodies with nutritious fuel.

Most Sunday evenings, we entertained the Gibsons (or maybe they entertained us). They dropped in almost without fail around suppertime. Mr. Gibson was a little older than Dad and was one of the regular weekday visitors at Dad's blacksmith shop and service station. Mom would invite them to stay for supper; thought they would politely refuse, they could easily be persuaded to stay.

The tantalizing bakery smell wafting through the house drew us to the dining room. Mom and Dad seated themselves at each end of the table with Mr. Gibson and my sister Josie on one side, me and Mrs. Gibson on the other. Mom served plenty of her just-out-of-the-oven, light-as-air baking-powder biscuits with lots of soft creamy butter and her homemade elderberry jelly. Mrs. Gibson always raved and raved as she enjoyed each bite of Mom's to-die-for biscuits and jelly.

Mr. Gibson, a short stocky man with a bald head and large wet lips, tried to give Josie a kiss at each visit but couldn't quite catch her. Josie and I viewed him as a funny little man, always wearing a wrinkled three-piece brown tweed suit. One time as he was telling one of his many oft-repeated stories (with gestures), Josie started to giggle silently and gave me the eye that said "look at his vest." There hung a little cotton ball from his ear, dangling on a fiber from one of the high points on his vest and moving in rhythm with his gestures. We fought back the urge to break out into hysterical laughter. Needless to say, Mom's Sunday evening suppers were always a hit.

At each visit, Mr. Gibson showed interest in the progress of my building projects, most often the bunks (forts) I built with my friends in our back yard. I would give him a detailed report that ended with "but the roof leaks." At each visit he mentioned he had a partly-used roll of tarpaper somewhere in his garage. He never did find that tarpaper, and the roof of our bunk always leaked.

Mom was popular in my school's Parent Teacher Association (PTA). I remember her ability to put on stunning promotional suppers, organizing and managing all the ladies who helped. She personally visited each table the night of the event to make sure everything ran smoothly. For a number of years, Dad served as treasurer for my school, Upper Moreland High School in Willow Grove. Mom did all his bookkeeping. The small stipend they received helped meet expenses at home. They were well respected in the school and community.

I am grateful for my mother's spirituality. She had personal devotions with her Bible open every morning. And she listened regularly to favorite radio Bible teachers. When I was quite little, my mother would remind me, "God's watching you, Paul. Don't lie. Always tell the truth. And be the best little boy you can possibly be." I tried, but many times I didn't measure up. I often experienced guilt and keenly felt the disappointment I figured I was causing Mother, myself and God.

But Mother also possessed a stubborn, authoritative streak — especially on medical issues. She would go to the doctor when we insisted she go, but afterward would take the medicine the way she thought best. She had a cabinet full of partly-filled medicine bottles and would often try to help folks by dispensing her medicines to them.

Unfortunately, this way of thinking was her demise. In her early '70s, a stone kicked up by my dad's lawn mower hit her ankle and caused a sore that would not heal (factor in probable diabetes by that age). Because she ignored her doctor's advice, the severe infection later sent her to the hospital where her leg was amputated. At the hospital, she suffered a stroke and never fully recovered from the physical or emotional trauma. She passed away at the age of 75.

Dad and the Shop

Shortly after my parents married, they moved to Willow Grove, and Dad left the Reading Railroad Company to start his own business repairing cars. He rented a building in the little, well-to-do town of Wyncote, near Jenkintown and about five miles south of Willow Grove. Gifted in auto mechanics, Dad enjoyed repairing cars and trucks. In time, he also became an Apperson Automobile Dealer.

Due to the success of Dad's business — prior to the Stock Market Crash in 1929 — he used savings to build an extensive new shop on Glenside Avenue, about two blocks away from his previous site. He added Gulf Standard and No-Knox gasoline pumps and offered Pennsylvania State Inspections. His big building sat back from the avenue and had a large paved u-shaped drive with the pumps set close to the building. A wide high door to the shop allowed easy access for servicing small trucks and Beaver College buses. (A few years later, he would add the blacksmith forge.)

One day at the shop, Dad told me he had to go to the post office, and I

Dad's shop included the forge, machine shop, front punch press and two blacksmithing vices, plus lots of room inside to park cars. The Sebastian Service Station was on Glenside Avenue in Wyncote.

should not try to satisfy any customers until he got back. He said he wouldn't be gone long, and he made a specific point of telling me not to sell any gas.

Just after he left, two elderly ladies drove up in their Model A Ford and stopped in front of the Gulf Standard gas pump. They wore flowered hats, though they reminded me of two old school teachers. I put on a smile and trotted out to see what they wanted.

The driver said, "Five gallons, please." I immediately recalled Dad's admonition not to sell any gas. I was just big enough that when Dad let me pump gas into his car, I had to stand on tiptoe to reach the crank at the top of the pump. I guessed Dad thought I was too little and weak. I'd show him! Here was a customer ready to spend money, and we needed sales. I wanted to prove myself to Dad, so why not take care of this transaction?

Pumping gas was hard work, but it seemed a lot easier that day. I thought to myself, I must be getting stronger. After I pumped the five gallons, the ladies paid me and off they went down Glenside Avenue.

A bit later, Dad returned and asked why I was grinning from ear to ear. I handed over the money and told him my story. He shook his head, and said, "Son, you didn't sell five gallons of gas, you sold five gallons of air. We don't have any gas in the tank today."

Oh, my! I felt terribly bad for the ladies, but we never saw them again.

Dad's Blacksmithing

I loved hearing Dad tell me about how he came to be a blacksmith.

Sometime close to my birth, a big brawny Englishman had stopped at Dad's shop to talk to him. Sam, a master blacksmith, said he wanted to relocate his forge to the Jenkintown-Wyncote area and needed a place where someone could care for him whenever he had epileptic seizures.

I was always fascinated when Dad talked about Sam's epileptic fits. Apparently he could have chewed off his tongue during convulsions! Terribly interesting for a little boy.

Sam's illness was terminal, and he told Dad he didn't think he had much time left to live. He asked Dad that day if he could set up his forging business in a section of Dad's large shop and, in exchange, he would teach Dad his trade in the time he had left. When he passed, everything would be Dad's property. Dad agreed to the deal, and looked forward to learning smithing from the old master.

What is it like to be a blacksmith? The day begins by lighting a small pile of wood shavings set upon a bed of high quality smithing coal in a fire-brick forge. Soon a sulfur smell accompanies thick smoke flowing up the forge's blackened chimney. The attached bellows are used to shoot air into the fire, increasing the temperature to about 2,000° F. Then work can begin.

The smith draws his design with chalk or soapstone on his iron leveling table. After stabbing a rod of wrought iron into the burning soft-coal, he waits, pumping the bellows to increase the temperature of the fire, and watching the color of the metal as it heats. He pulls the metal out of the coals just far enough to observe its color. Dark orange or red metal is too cool and resistant to hammer blows; the metal is ready for shaping when it is glowing yellow, almost clay-like and easily formed. The smith places the hot metal on his anvil and sends sparks and metal scale (dust and flakes) flying as he precisely pounds it into the required object.

Sam and Dad worked together for several years before Sam died and Dad was on his own. The smithing business joined Dad's machine shop, car dealership and gas station. This worked in Dad's favor when the Great Depression hit us just after Sam passed away.

Cherry Street

Dad created a business card (left) for the Laseco Forge
and imprinted the company name, date and town on his pieces (right).

Not too long before I was born, Uncle Walter loaned my parents the $5,000 required to purchase their home on Cherry Street. The house was half a double, so another family usually lived on the other side. The house was built in such a way that the floorboards were the very same boards on both sides, and acted as highways for the neighbors' friendly roaches. On rainy days, the kids next door would roller skate through their side of the house, and we could hear and feel the vibrations on our side. The other half of our duplex had many occupants over the years; some of whom moved out in the middle of the night to skip paying their rent. In spite of these things, growing up on Cherry Street was just right for me.

Only one block long, our street was inhabited by about a hundred kids of all ages. Many of us played street hockey from curb to curb on four-wheel clamp-on roller skates. Anyone could become a player simply by buying a hockey stick at the hardware store. You could always pick out other hockey players by checking for scabbed knees. We also rode bicycles and homemade go-carts, built "bunks" (our name for playhouses or bunkhouses) and played baseball.

Our half of the duplex on Cherry Street

Cherry Street boasted its own baseball diamond. Sure the field was covered with a lot of overgrown weeds, but it wasn't all that bad. The weeds slowed down the ground balls so we didn't have to chase them nearly as far. We never had enough players for one team, let alone two teams for a regular game. So, we played "movers-up." After deciding who would bat first, the rest of us would take positions in the infield and outfield. If the batter got on base, all players would move to the next lower base, and so forth until you got to bat. After you crossed home plate, you'd play the field again. It was tons of fun and gave us practice at each position.

The street began with the rather famous (or was it infamous?) Cherry Street Bar at the Route 611 end. The only time my parents ever allowed me to go into the bar was to deliver newspapers as a high schooler, which is when I saw all the bottles of alcohol and pictures of very scantily clothed women. The other end led to Route 63 with Johnny Radcliff's store on the corner.

At Johnny's you could buy bread, milk, cold cuts, candy, ice cream, and some fresh vegetables—if you had any money, that is. It was owned and operated by Johnny, an old bachelor who lived across Route 63 with his two spinster sisters. When he went home at noon for lunch, one of his sisters would run the store until he returned. No one wanted to visit during Johnny's lunch hour, because the sisters were crabby and stingy, especially to kids. They acted like they owned the place and treated us like we didn't matter much.

I happened to be at the store one day during Johnny's lunch break. The lady in line ahead of me had a conversation going with one of the sisters, "...and weren't you ever married?"

The sister immediately snapped, "Certainly not! No man ever took advantage of me." I got the idea she did not trust men, or anyone for that

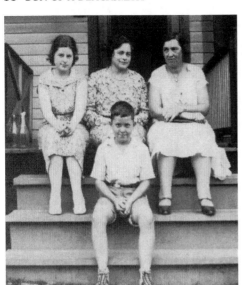

Joining me on our front porch:
Josie, Mom and (her sister) Aunt Lily.

matter. I felt sorry for her because she seemed so unhappy.

Johnny's store was usually filled with people. A potbelly stove in the middle of the store kept customers warm in the winter. Men from the neighborhood used to sit around the stove and spin yarns. One time, I heard retired Mr. Carthouser complaining about bankers having short banking hours. Johnny put an end to that conversation by grumbling, "You can't complain; you take 365 days off every year now." This brought a chuckle from everyone and effectively silenced Mr. Carthouser. I really enjoyed hearing the stories the old fellows told — and now I am one myself.

During the Great Depression, no one had much money, sometimes not even enough for food. Understanding this, Johnny kindly gave people full-measure-plus for the little money we had to spend. One time I remember asking for five cents worth of pretzels. He took the glass lid off the big pretzel can and completely filled a big brown paper bag. Sometimes when I had a penny for candy, he exhibited great patience waiting for my decision. I generally ended up choosing six licorice babies or eight green spearmint leaves, since with care they might last all day.

Next to Johnny's was a blacksmith's shop. Kids were prohibited from entering, but we watched from a distance, mesmerized by the heat of the fire, the smell of hot iron and the clang of the anvil with the blow of the hammer. We learned a few things as the smithy made shoes and nailed them to hooves of the street merchant's horses — and picked up a few choice words as well. I particularly remember the ability of the smithy to recognize a solution to a problem. One time he attached a bracket to a horseshoe so the horse would stop routinely turning its ankle. A smell I found repugnant was caused by the hot iron shoe burning its imprint into the horse's hoof as the smithy attached it.

A blacksmith who trims and shoes horses' hooves is technically called a farrier. My dad was a blacksmith also, but he was the type that crafts useful and decorative items from wrought iron. Like a farrier, he also used a forge, hammer and anvil; however, there was an interesting difference between their anvils. The farrier used a "live" anvil that rang with a ping, ping, ping like a high-pitched bell as he shaped a horseshoe. Dad's Fisher anvil was a "dead" anvil because it had a heavy steel plate atop that deadened the sound and extended the life of the anvil. The size and shape of the two anvils was also quite different. The farrier's anvil had a short, wide working deck with a stubby horn, just right for forming shoes. Dad's anvil had an elongated steel deck with a long heavy horn necessary for more intricate objects (like scrolls) and for larger work.

Once in a while Mom would send me a block or so over to the Willow Grove Bakery to buy half a dozen right-out-of-the-oven crumb buns. The short, stout German baker had a heavy accent, and she always greeted me with, "Hello! My stuff is so 'goot.'" Truly, every bakery item was delectable.

Many things happened right there on Cherry Street. Every week a variety of vendors visited us. The rag man paid by the pound for our rags no matter how bad their condition. His old horse always looked incapable of taking another step. The scissors man sharpened scissors and knives right there on our sidewalk. The trash man collected waste once a week, and the garbage man came twice each week. On hot summer days, we couldn't wait until he moved on up the street. Each vendor would yell or chant their identity to get attention and let people know he was coming down the street and ready to serve you. Hearing vendors was not a problem, since home air conditioning had not yet been invented. On Cherry Street, everyone's windows were open for the duration of the summer.

The door-to-door bread man and the milk man would let Mom run up a bill that she'd pay in full when Dad could bring home some money. When Dad returned from work each day, he entered the house at the kitchen door and gave Mom a big kiss as she was cooking our dinner. Mom would always ask, "How did we do today, Jim?"

I vividly recall the night he shook his head and replied, "Just fifteen cents worth of gas, Mary."

Mom replied, "Oh, Jim! What are we going to do?" And they hugged for a long time.

And so, as a young boy, I learned the value of credit and the worry of not having enough money to pay your bills.

But much of my life as a kid was simply fun! On a hot summer day, we kids loved to follow the iceman down Cherry Street because it was so refreshing. He made a delivery at almost every house. From a huge 300-pound master block,

As a little fellow, my favorite ladies were Mom, Aunt Alta, Josie and Aunt Josephine (pictured in our Cherry Street living room).

he would chop off a 30-pound block of ice, run with it to a lady's back door, and put it in her ice box for just fifteen cents. When he left his wagon, we'd scramble in the back and find a nice-size chip to enjoy. He yelled at us, but we kept our distance and repeated our quest for another chip at a later stop. That ice was better than candy.

My Favorite Aunt, Uncle and Cousin

Of all my relatives, I loved visiting Dad's brother Walter's family and saw them often. Uncle Walt had married Alta Cooper, a genteel lady who completed finishing school (teaching that focuses on social graces and etiquette) in Richmond, Virginia, where her father was pastor of the Richmond Baptist Church. Walt and Alta had two children, Walter, Jr. (who died as a young child; see photo in Appendix B) and George. Although seven years older, my cousin George treated me like a favored younger brother.

The family was very well-to-do. Uncle Walt was a gentleman farmer; he neither kept animals nor planted crops. As the chief civil engineer of the Reading Railroad, he went to his office in Philadelphia daily, Monday through Friday. But he also worked hard and was industrious around the farm. He rented out his open fields, and he maintained 50 or so cabins that were situated around the meadow adjacent to Neshaminy Creek. He rented out the cabins during the summer to vacationers who came through the area.

George was average height and slender (compared to me), and he had a million-dollar smile. He was easy-going and had a great understanding of how things work. His bright mind always reached for ways to do things more easily.

To my delight, two different years (when I was twelve and thirteen), I got to spend an unforgettable summer week at the farm. Over the years George introduced me to many fascinating inventions, projects and hobbies. One thing I loved immediately was photography — both camera and darkroom

My first swim – in the Neshaminy Creek, wearing the most modern of bathing suits
(a hand-me-down from George).

technology—which would later become part of my career path and a life-long passion.

Aunt Alta knew her way around every possible social situation. She ran her household very pleasantly and efficiently. Miss Standish, an elderly genteel English lady and dear friend of my Aunt Alta, lived with the family for many years. She helped Aunt Alta cook and was always seated with us at Aunt Alta's delicious dinners. Aunt Alta also trained one of the girls from the local village of Scottsville to clean house, help in the kitchen and serve dinner. She was a lovely girl named Emma.

Every morning after the breakfast dishes were washed and put away, Aunt Alta called everyone into the living room where we read the Bible aloud and prayed together. They always skipped me (because I couldn't read fluently and couldn't

George was a great friend to Josie, too; they were almost the same age.

pronounce some of the words) but never let me feel embarrassed about it.

Large and sumptuous meals graced Aunt Alta's table day in and day out, where she sat at one end of the dining table and Uncle Walter at the other, with guests and Miss Standish in between. The guest of honor (if there was one) sat at Aunt Alta's right hand.

Before the meal, Uncle Walter prayed, thanking God for the food and asking His blessing upon it. Then he would stand to carve the roast over a stack of warmed dinner plates. Next, Aunt Alta would ask each of us to pick up a serving dish near us, usually filled with piping hot mashed potatoes or a variety of vegetables in cream sauce or right-out-of-the-oven dinner rolls with butter and jam. The only thing better than her dinners were her desserts, served with coffee or milk. Every meal at their home was fit for a king.

The only dinner that could top Aunt Alta's regular fare was her Thanksgiving Feast, to which my family was invited year after year. If my Upper Moreland's football team won the annual game with Hatboro, it was an extra-perfect day. As part of the marching band, I remember being frightfully cold in regular white pants and white shirt with a band cape and hat. After the game, I warmed my frozen self in front of Uncle Walt's walk-in fireplace in the dining room. The wood burning fireplaces throughout the farmhouse crackled and popped and generously gave us the heat that felt so good. With a delicious dinner aroma emanating from the kitchen, I felt right at home.

After I warmed up, my cousin George would usher me off to his hobby room to show me his newest inventions, drawings and interests. By the time I was in high school, George was attending the University of Pennsylvania studying electrical engineering. A top student, George had attended Meadowbrook, a private grammar school, then been prepared for college at Penn Charter, a college prep school.

When called for dinner, we entered the dining room where the big table

Uncle Walter's walk-in fireplace in his 1810 farmhouse crackled, popped and gave delicious heat in winter.

was covered with a perfectly pressed white tablecloth. A full set of silverware with extra company-only utensils, crystal water goblet, small dish of applesauce and bread plate with ball of butter sat at each person's place. The Thanksgiving Turkey, browned and plump with tasty filling, sat in front of Uncle Walt. His prayer expressed sincere appreciation to God for salvation, health, strength and family. Then he asked each guest what cut of turkey they preferred, carved it, placed the meat on a warmed plate and passed it to them. I always asked for a drumstick. The rest of the menu consisted of fluffy mashed potatoes with pools of butter and a sprinkle of paprika for color, cauliflower, pearl onions, and peas...some of the vegetables were covered with a cream sauce, and freshly baked rolls with butter and homemade preserves—very lovely and tasty. After a leisurely dinner, home-baked desserts were served along with fresh coffee for the grownups.

George, forever inventing, saw a need for his mother to summon Emma from the kitchen when she needed something. So, he installed a door bell button under the carpet near Aunt Alta's right foot. By stepping on the hump in the carpet, Aunt Alta could buzz Emma to come to the table and see what Aunt Alta needed. Initially Aunt Alta buzzed Emma accidentally several times, but finally figured out how to avoid stepping on the button by mistake. (And I'm delighted to say that George's inventing rubbed off on me!)

Aunt Alta and Uncle Walter were active in their church and often invited the young people to their farm for socials. I remember a watermelon party they hosted where I made a pig of myself, eating far too much juicy watermelon and creamy potato salad. In the middle of the night in my guest room, I woke up in a cold sweat, stomach heaving. I desperately tried to get to the bathroom but didn't even quite make it to the door. Hearing the commotion, Uncle Walt came to my aid, helping me back to bed and cleaning up the mess. Next morning, I apologized, and he just kindly smiled.

I did love my aunt's cooking and baking. As a special treat, she would often make me my special Gee Whiz Cake (*see recipe in Appendix C*). Like a huge, inch-high gingerbread cookie, it was loaded with nuts and Muscats, extra-large raisins — it didn't need any icing. I can remember the spicy aroma of that warm cake, served with a glass of cold milk – a treat I was ready for any time. (In tasting the prepared recipe as we wrote this book, I realized even taste buds have memory.)

Junior League and the Tom Thumb Wedding

Many times during the Great Depression, we couldn't afford gas to drive to our church in Fox Chase. So, Mom would send me just a block away to the Willow Grove Methodist Church on Sundays. And I went to Junior League Boys Club on Friday afternoons. Mom was well known to the ladies at the Methodist church because of her activities and productions at the Willow Grove public schools. She always took pleasure in heading up PTA dinners and benefit affairs, and groups were always delighted for her help.

One day Mom told me she had been asked to help with a fundraiser for the Methodist Church, a "Tom Thumb Wedding." Staging a Tom Thumb wedding, in which all of the wedding roles were generally played by children under ten, was an American fad from the '20s to the '70s. This would be a reenactment of a real-life event that occurred in 1863. General Tom Thumb (born Charles Stratton) never grew more than about three feet tall and was a circus celebrity championed by P.T. Barnum who named him after the folk hero Tom Thumb. Tom's marriage in New York City to Lavinia Warren, another little person, had attracted national attention.

The only wedding I had ever attended was when my cousin Lillian married Clarence Erwin. I had been all of six. I asked Mom if the church would have good food like at Lillian's wedding reception. She assured me they would. She said the church ladies had asked her to help them with all the details, and she went on to describe how everything would take place. I would wear a special suit called a tuxedo which she was going to make. Mom assured me several times that wedding ushers don't talk, and I felt good about that.

A Tom Thumb wedding was a big event for Willow Grove. We were the first in the little town of 5,000 to put one on. Tickets sold out fast. The whole thing was a benefit for something the church needed, but I can't remember what.

I learned that everyone in the play were participants in the church's Sunday School or Junior League. I was about six years old, but many of the kids were younger and shorter than I. Even the wedding guest actors were little kids, and I was to usher them to their seats. I was not required to say a word, and that was fine with me.

The creation of my tuxedo was coming along fine. I remember looking at myself in the full-length mirror. I thought, "Wow! I think I'm going to like this." My shoes were supposed to be patent leather, but I only had one pair — a shabby brown — and they would have to do. Other than that, I was ready for the dress rehearsal.

The men of the church had created an elevated runway of sorts over some of the pews so everyone could see the processional. The walkway had no railings, and the fear of falling overboard was ever-present, because the boards were not very well secured. And I never did like heights. At the rehearsal, the ladies and Mom told us in detail every move we should make. We repeated each part over and over again until everyone was pleased. The kids with talking parts had to go over and over and over their lines. A taller kid played the part of the preacher. He did a great job. I did not care for the practice. I had no lines and understood my roles, so I was ready.

At the "wedding," the church was packed and we ushers were told to start seating the wedding guests. All went well. The bride and her father (an older, taller boy) waited for the wedding march to begin. The church organist played since no kid was allowed to touch the organ. Then the preacher, the groom and his men (boys) watched from the front as the bride and her dad approached.

After the groom promised to take care of the bride, the preacher gave a very short sermon. Finally, guests followed the bride and groom to the reception room for cake and ice cream. The cake was cut in skimpy pieces accompanied by only a spoonful of ice cream. But I figured that was okay since it was a very small wedding (although I could have handled more).

All the actors received congratulations, and I got quite a few compliments on my tuxedo. With all this, and not losing anyone off the runway — although I had thought about it — I figured this was a successful event. It was definitely the beginning and the ending of my life's acting career.

I would have rather been playing baseball.

And so passed my carefree early years, until the confinement of school.

Chapter 2

Grade School

In fear and trembling, I began first grade. I was five and could have waited until the next school year, but Mother talked the administrator into admitting me early. I didn't like the idea. Why go there when I could have endlessly entertained myself without it? But there I was, walking the three blocks to Davisville Road Elementary School of the Upper Moreland School District in Willow Grove.

Adventures in First Grade

I now fondly remember Mrs. Jamieson, my first-grade teacher, who turned out to be quite fun and a great reader of stories. She read Robinson Crusoe with different voices for each character, nurturing in me a great love for stories (if they were read or told to me).

In this first grade class picture from Davisville Grammar School,
I am standing fourth from the left in the back row between two girls.

Another source of listening to stories was radio, all the rage in those years before television was invented. Getting home from school in the later afternoon, I tuned in to *The Singing Lady* who sang and told stories using a variety of character voices. *Stella Dallas* came next but didn't interest me much because it was about girls and women. Activating my imagination, I enjoyed the dramatic programs best. *Uncle Don* used a prototype tear-shaped vehicle that bypassed roads, navigating across water and fields. The famous *Buck Rodgers of the 25th Century* mesmerized me, and also appeared in comic books and action stories. *The Lone Ranger* (with his faithful sidekick Tonto) never failed to captivate me. Other action programs like *Jack Armstrong, the All-American Boy, The Easy Aces, Mr. Keen: Tracer of Lost Persons* and *Tom Mix* were programs I never missed.

Aunt Alta somehow learned about my fascination with *Tom Mix*, a cowboy movie and radio character who stopped train robbers and rescued damsels. On the program, they offered a realistic six-shooter with wooden bullets, holster and gun belt. You could get this by sending in 75 Ralston cereal box tops. Unfortunately, my family ate only cornflakes. However, because my aunt told her prayer circle ladies to save Ralston box tops for me, I was able to send off for the pistol.

Waiting for my pistol to arrive was both excruciating and exhilarating. I ran home from school every day at noon to check the morning mail. The day it arrived, I had a difficult time returning to school for the afternoon. The pistol only shot the distance of about five feet, but that was okay with me.

Once in Mrs. Jamieson's first grade, I experienced a very bad day at school, though I can't for the life of me remember what caused my foul mood. Upon returning home, I recall my mother being too busy with her work to give me her normal cheerful greeting. I was down-in-the-dumps grumpy.

When Mom finished whatever she was doing and asked how school went, I don't know why I said it, but I did: "My teacher beat me." The lie hung in the air.

Before I could take a breath, Mother was rapidly walking me back to school. Marching into the building, she grabbed me by the hand and walked me toward Miss Jamison's room (a nicer teacher you will never find).

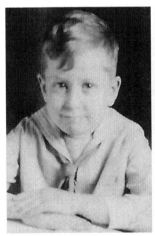

My first, third and sixth grade "mugshots."

I immediately admitted to my mother and teacher: "I lied, and I'm very sorry." My face was red...and soon my bottom matched.

Mom had a way of making herself understood. She didn't say much on our way home, but I recall her clipped words, "Wait 'til your father hears about this." I'm sure she was embarrassed, too.

When Dad got home, he listened to Mother's story and then took me into the dining room. Instead of an additional spanking, I received a lecture I still remember telling me how awful it is to lie, that it is very ungodly and that I must always tell the truth. I learned an unforgettable lesson that day.

The Great Depression

I was five when the Stock Market collapsed on October 29, 1929, marking the beginning of the Great Depression. Banks everywhere—including Dad's, the Jenkintown Citizens National Bank—closed without refunding anyone's money. Panic swept our nation. Most companies went out of business, and men everywhere were suddenly without work. Poverty became the way of life for many years until our nation began preparing for World War II.

My family lost all our savings in the bank collapse. Dad came home from the bank that last time, shaking his head and repeating over and over, "I put my money in a safe place...the Citizens National Bank...it seemed so safe..."

We were relatively poor, but the Lord met our needs every day. Our local newspaper ran photographs of devastation around the country, but I did not feel it as much as most people. Etched into my memory, however, is one photo of a soup kitchen with lines and lines of men waiting for food. I thank God that was not our reality because of Dad's business ventures.

We always had enough food, thanks also in part to my mother's resourcefulness. She had an excellent business sense and squirreled away money whenever she could. In times of real need, she would turn up the rug and find a dollar bill, or look in a canister and find a few nickels. In those days, five cents could buy a loaf of bread or bag of pretzels. 20 cents would get you a dozen eggs.

Mom packed a daily lunch for Dad that consisted of—without fail—four elderberry jelly sandwiches. She also packed two identical sandwiches in a little brown bag for me to take to school. One day I inadvertently picked up the wrong brown bag, bit into a lard sandwich and thought I would be sick. It was disgusting! Boy, was I relieved when the teacher found my lunch. It gave me pause to realize that lard between bread was all some kids had to eat in those perilous times.

Aunt Alta gave us clothes that George had outgrown, and Mom would make them over to fit me. I guess I was rather unaware of our poverty; nor did I notice that I lacked for anything.

Every summer we had a backyard vegetable garden with string beans, lima beans, Golden Bantam corn, peas... Beside our garden, I kept about 20 chickens in a pen. I enjoyed tending the chickens, especially the baby chicks. Mother would give some eggs to our relatives, but we consumed most of them ourselves or they were used in her baking. Occasionally we would eat one of the young chickens, which was okay with me. I thought they were very dumb

I took pride in my chickens.

animals—they could get out of the fence but not find their way back in.

During the Great Depression, Dad's business and entrepreneurial ventures barely made enough money to support the family. The start of World War II created a great number of employment opportunities and began reviving the US economy. In 1940, Dad gave up the shop and got a good, steady job at the Philadelphia Navy Yard and sometimes had the opportunity to work overtime. We gave the Lord thanks for the many ways He provided for us during the most difficult times.

Reading Challenges

As a young child, I loved to listen to books being read to me aloud. Reading them myself was an altogether different story.

Mom, an avid reader, insisted during my grade school years on reading all of my homework to me. She wrote my papers, too. She loved me *too* much in that way. And she unwittingly fostered a reading weakness in me that eventually required a no-credit, Basic English class at Penn State University.

I wonder, looking back on my own daughter's early reading problems, if I may have had similar difficulties that frustrated my mother. In those days, schools did not test or give extra support to children with learning challenges. Mom was most likely coping the best way she knew how as she read to me and "helped" me work on my assignments. I know she wanted the best for me in every way.

One of my reading milestones happened when Miss Price, my pretty fourth grade teacher, started a Library in our school. Everyone in her class had to choose a book to read. I faced a daunting task. Looking at all the books on the shelves, I chose a small book with few words in large type and lots of pictures about a boy in Africa. Actually reading a whole book by myself gave me a grand sense of victory. I did it!

Jumping ahead on the topic of reading, I can say that not all milestones were quite so positive. In sixth grade, I sat in Miss Mays' home room. I hated her geography class, because every day she required students to stand up and read-aloud a paragraph or so from our book. She almost always called on us alphabetically, starting with Neal Akers. Because my last name is Sebastian, the bell always ended the class before my turn.

One particular day, she began choosing students from the end of the alphabet. When she got to the Ss, I was trapped! She called my name. Doomsday had arrived.

I scrambled to my feet with my heavy geography book in my sweaty hands, heart thumping, and began to read. I did my best, carefully picking through the words until I got to "island." I pronounced it "is-land."

Now Miss Mays never was a pleasant person. My classmates and I concurred that she must have hated teaching. That day I felt like she hated me.

Her piercing voice cut into my concentration: "That's 'island,' Paul. Your reading is miserable. *Sit down and don't ever get up again!*"

Snickers sounded around the room. I was crushed. My secret was out. I felt like I was going to die at age twelve, mortified at being such a failure in front of my classmates.

That day I became afraid of the sound of my own voice. Over 80 years later, I still experience difficulty reading aloud on any occasion. Throughout the years, I dismissed many valuable opportunities due to this phobia.

Case in point, during my military experience, a captain encouraged me to apply for officer training at West Point. This sixth-grade incident immediately flashed into my mind, and I pictured myself standing before the cadets reading an order about an island and calling it an "is-land." I thanked my captain for his kind recommendation but satisfied myself with my sergeant's rank.

Miss Mays inadvertently taught me the terrible power of critical words — not something in her teacher's job description to be sure, but very effective nonetheless.

Bullies

In my early school years, I remember Mother asking me, as I returned home each day, "How did school go?" She liked to hear all the details.

I soon tired of that daily questioning. After all, school was over for the day, and I just wanted to go out and play baseball with my buddies. I began saying, "Everybody kissed me today." *She* tired of that response and insisted on more information.

I only ever spoke about good things that happened; I never told her I was bullied almost every day. In truth, bullying was part of every first-grade recess.

A pipe fence with a loose top rail stood in an unsupervised back section of our playground. Bullies would push the smaller, weaker first grade boys into the fence and squeeze the rail down over them, effectively trapping, humiliating and even hurting them.

Taswell, a big, black kid, ruled the playground as king of the bullies. Everyone feared Taswell — even me, though I tried not to show it.

I was never quite sure how a shy, timid white kid like me became his buddy, but Taswell took a liking to me. From that point forward, the other tough kids basically left me alone. Standing in Taswell's protective shadow, I welcomed the relief of his self-appointed guardianship as the other small kids tried to escape the playground horrors.

One day after school ended, Taswell came around the corner of the building and noticed I was being threatened by some of his friends. He kicked my nemesis in the backside with each step the bully took as he tried to flee from Taswell.

I believe he intimidated even the teachers. It sounds silly, but I don't know that he ever graduated from first grade! He never seemed to do any work, and sometimes we could hear him walking around in the attic of the school. Our teacher would glance up, shake her head, and go on with the lesson. Taswell just kept getting bigger and bigger and remained in first grade year after year.

I've wondered more than once what happened to him in the ensuing years. I am forever grateful for his protective influence.

School Friends

Although I can remember many classmates between first and twelfth grades, my closest school friends were Frances Payne, John Geckler and Jack Raiser. Especially memorable was an annual Christmas party our mothers arranged so we could play with our new Christmas toys. The moms served us delicious sandwiches, an array of Christmas cookies, and hot chocolate with real whipped cream. We all looked forward to this special time every year. And the four of us enjoyed many escapades throughout our school years.

One day in grade school, I enjoyed an unscheduled event—a hike in the woods—made possible because the school was suddenly uninhabitable due to a horrific stink later identified as Limburger cheese placed on a stream-heated radiator. We students were thrilled to be outside all day. Later I realized the culprit was John Geckler, one of my close buddies. Although he never got caught, several of us figured it had to be him. He was smart: smart enough to know the prank would stink enough to get us out of school, and smart enough to get away with doing it. His father, a scientist who worked for the government, had taught John something about chemistry by that early age.

Many years later Jean and I visited John at his home in Yakima, Washington, during a trip across the Canadian Rockies. He was lead surgeon at

On Cherry Street in Willow Grove, my best friend Jimmy Cunningham (far right) and I built this snow cave in his front yard when we were about six. Also pictured are Jimmy's sister Mildred (in the cave) and Andy Rowe (beside Mildred).

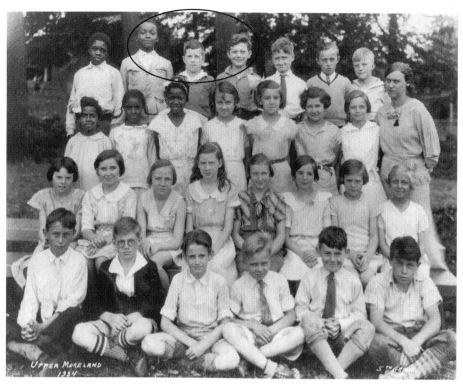

In this fifth grade class photo, I am third from the left in the back row.
Two best friends stand on either side of me, Frank Smith and John Geckler.

Several years ago I visited Frank Smith in his Maine home where we enjoyed reminiscing about
the good old days. He had earned his Ph.D. and taught college for many years.

Yakima General Hospital, and their daughter was a nurse at Lancaster General Hospital (a major hospital in the city where Jean and I reside today—what a coincidence!). We stayed overnight with John and his wife, Charlotte. She served us a home-cooked fresh salmon dinner that was so delicious I remember asking for seconds. I now regret not bringing up the Limburger story, which could have brought quite a laugh and perhaps more remembrances.

Several weeks after writing the first draft of this chapter, I remembered an additional detail. The Limburger cheese incident took place in Miss Mays' classroom. The more I think about those years, the more I recall her cold and unkind ways, realizing the incredibly negative impact she had on all her students—not just me. This has created in me a deep gratitude for other wise and compassionate teachers who encouraged me throughout my life.

An Introduction to Architectural Drawing and Building

My first drawing project probably goes back to the age of six. I remember being intrigued with a picture of the Queen Mary ocean liner in my father's National Geographic Magazine. I began drawing the ship on a long piece of kitchen shelf paper that covered most of the dining room table. Dad passed by as I was working and tugged on my cowlick, asking, "Son, can you draw your breath?" Ha! The Queen Mary was such a big project I am not sure I ever finished it. Yet this drawing represented the beginning of my engineering career.

My yen for building came somewhere around the fifth grade. I would scrounge all the wood I could from around the neighborhood, whatever had no owner. With the wood, my buddies and I built "bunks"—clubhouses, for boys only!—in my backyard. We would often salvage and straighten old nails to use, but sometimes Mom would give me a nickel to go to Nichols' Hardware and buy some nails. Mr. Nichols never weighed it, and I always thought he gave me more than my nickel's worth.

Jimmy Cunningham, Jimmy McIntyre, Jimmy McGarvey, Gordon Caldwell and others made up our boys' club of sorts. They would meet me in my

Photo continues on next page. This massive cathedral door hinge took Dad 400 hours to sculpt during the Great Depression in the early '30s. Designer Bill Hare, prominent Philadelphia architect, lost the bid for the cathedral work, so Dad's weeks of work ...

backyard to build a bunk. Since we could not afford tarpaper to cover the roof, our bunks leaked when it rained. I often wished for the tarpaper Mr. Gibson kept promising. However, we had great fun with our building projects.

Jimmy Cunningham was my very closest friend on Cherry Street. He lived about six houses down the street from me. During the summer Jimmy and I were almost always together. He was game to join me in my latest project, like the time we decided to have our own circus. Jimmy raised fancy pigeons and I had a Pointer (dog). Out of scrap wood, we built a cage over my express wagon and put Pal inside. We rallied some other kids who brought pets and flags...and we all marched down Cherry Street yelling, "Come to the Circus." That was the extent of the circus idea; it was fun while it lasted but didn't work, like many of our harebrained schemes.

Jimmy attended St. David's Parochial School in Willow Grove for eight years. When his folks sent him to the big Catholic high school in Philadelphia, we lost touch. In recent years we enjoyed lunch together and talked many hours about the adventures of our youth. He passed away about three years ago, and I miss our reminiscing.

Dad's Iron Work

The arrangement between Sam (the English blacksmith I mentioned in Chapter 1) and my dad worked well in the pre-Depression years. Dad caught on steadily and progressed rapidly in mastering the art of fine metal smithing. By the time Sam died, Dad was well on his way to becoming a master blacksmith, discovered by two architects who began to regularly hire him for satisfying and lucrative jobs.

These jobs, however, dropped off almost completely when the Depression hit. Most folks—even the well-to-do—couldn't afford gated wrought iron fences around their properties. But there were smaller jobs and practical items that kept Dad busy.

Dad produced beautiful items of wrought iron. Fire place tools, screens and andirons, light sconces, floor lamps and chandeliers, candle sticks, latch and

...were for naught. Upon its return, Dad found modeling clay under the scales of the dragon, indicating it had been copied, presumably to be reproduced in cast iron. I've personally wondered what business a dragon has on a church door...

Dad forged this door latch (top L),
decorative hinge (top R)
and wall sconce (L).

Photo Credit: Keith Baum

hinge hardware, church door hinges, the list goes on and on. He became a very accomplished fine arts blacksmith, able to make almost anything out of wrought iron.

Dad's largest and most famous work is at the Washington National Cathedral in DC. In the late 1920s, Lawrence Saint, a famous stained glass artist was commissioned by the Cathedral to design the large Rose Window for the North Transept and several windows for their Children's Chapel. Along with my family, Saint was also a member of Bethany Baptist Church in Fox Chase. He knew Dad and the quality of his work. He saw to it that Dad was commissioned to design, build and install the wrought iron work for all the windows that held his stained glass securely in place.

The Rose Window was 21 feet in diameter, the largest of all the Cathedral's 215 stained glass windows, with more than 10,000 pieces of stained glass in the Rose window alone.

When the iron work was finished, it was shipped to the Cathedral and Dad went to Washington a week at a time to install his work. Each morning a crane would lift Dad to the high scaffolding with his oversized bottles of oxygen, acetylene and torch to assemble and weld the window sections together.

It was 1931 and I was in second grade when he completed the work. He took Mom and me (Josie had to stay in school) to Washington for his final week of the installation. Some of the time we looked up and watched him doing his work, except for welding. Other times we went sightseeing. I remember the Smithsonian very well, and also the wonderful food and very delicious cake at the fancy hotel.

During the summers I often went with Dad to work at his shop. I learned a lot about forging wrought iron. I was age 12 when Dad asked if I would like to try being his "striker" — that's the guy who stands in front of the anvil with a sledge hammer above his head to strike the smith's forming tools in the process of reshaping the red-hot iron. I eagerly said "yes" and got to work over the anvil. Forging was extremely heavy, dirty and hot work for a preteen, even though I began with a lighter sledge and had a sturdy wooden box to stand on.

At first I wasn't very accurate in hitting his tools, but I quickly got the hang of it.

Soon I was helping with lots of jobs. It was great fun to work with him. One process that intrigued me was making a forge-weld. This type of weld begins with tapering two pieces of iron with cherry red heat, then heating both again but to white heat, being very careful not to let the iron "burn." Next a little flux (fine sand or borax) is added, and then the pieces are pounded together again. This makes an even stronger weld than by using an acetylene torch to weld only around the edges.

The North Rose Window of the Washington National Cathedral (in color on the front cover), entitled "Last Judgment."

Dad's shop was fascinating to me as a young boy. It held a machine shop area with the big lathe and drill presses, all powered by an overhead leather belt system; the punch press which had its own motor; and two work benches made of heavy wooden timbers to which gigantic blacksmith's vices were fastened. Sam had maintained his equipment in excellent condition, and the forge even boasted an electric motor with a rheostat that powered the air-blower at various speeds to control the heat of the fire.

While working so close to the forge in Dad's shop, I had plenty of time and experience to be sure the extreme heat and dirt from pounding iron was not something I wanted to do for the rest of my life. I distinctly remember Dad taking me with him to visit the architects who designed many of the objects he made. I was mesmerized by their drawings *and* their nice clean offices. On the way home from one of those visits, I told Dad I'd rather be an architect than a blacksmith. He just smiled. Shortly after that, he asked me to design a large post light to illuminate the entrance yard just outside Uncle Walt's farm house. I learned I really did enjoy design work far more than the process of making the actual piece.

Visitors dropped by the shop all the time to talk and to watch Dad work. Some would ask questions and others made suggestions. He kindly answered

My dad James E. Sebastian is shown in formal pose (left) and portrayed (right) by artist Lawrence Saint in a sketch used in his St. John's Chapel stained-glass design in the Washington Cathedral.

The first item I designed in metal (during high school) was this post light Dad and I made in his shop for Uncle Walt's farm.

each one and explained the best way to solve each problem. He was patient with all, just a great guy. I was proud to call him my dad.

Even though Dad was a gifted artisan of iron, later I often thought that God not only gave him a great ability with his hands but also gave him wisdom, understanding and patience to know how to start a job and finish it to perfection. I believe he prayed much about his work, especially as he worked on important projects and when he came in contact with people he could talk to about the Lord.

Accepting the Savior

It turned out to be my Dad who prompted my salvation experience. Bethany Baptist was a Gospel-preaching, missionary-sending church. Reverend A. F. Ballbach, the pastor and a very loving man, faithfully taught God's Word. Some of our young people received God's call to serve on the mission field. One of the most notable was Lawrence Saint's son, Nate, from my Sunday School class. Nate Saint later became a famous missionary pilot who was murdered in 1956 by Auca Indians in Ecuador, South America.

Sunday nights Pastor Ballbach preached the Gospel and made it very clear that Jesus said everyone needed to born again. He always closed the service with an altar call inviting anyone who wanted to accept Jesus Christ as their personal Savior to walk forward and meet him at the altar.

As a 12-year-old, I felt the Holy Spirit's convicting presence every Sunday evening for nearly a year as the pastor issued the altar call. A timid kid—almost afraid of my shadow—I just couldn't make myself walk up there. I knew I was a sinner and deserved hell, a place I surely didn't want to go…but…

My 13th birthday came and went. I was a "striker," a photographer and a budding architect, but I still had not answered God's call. One night right after supper, Mom and Josie were in the kitchen washing dishes. I was ready to leave the dining room table to go down to my cellar darkroom, and Dad said, "Wait a minute, Son." Very directly and seriously he said, "When will you accept Jesus as your own personal Savior?"

I replied immediately, "Next Sunday night, Dad." And so I did just that and received Jesus in my heart on February 7, 1937. I felt like a new man, bound for Heaven to see Jesus. My salvation verse was John 3:16, "For God so loved the world that He gave His only begotten Son, that whoever believes in Him should not perish but have everlasting life."

A year later, I dedicated my life to God's service, according to Romans 12:1, "I beseech you therefore, brethren, by the mercies of God, that you present your bodies a living sacrifice, holy, acceptable to God, which is your reasonable service." Shortly afterwards I was baptized by Pastor Ballbach.

More About Visiting George

No matter my age or the occasion, time spent with Uncle Walter, Aunt Alta and George enriched my life. I looked forward to every encounter. One summer when I was about twelve, Aunt Alta invited me to stay with George for a whole week. Each day we would do something different. Most everything was new and fascinated me. He treated me as an equal even though he was seven years older.

George taught me to fish for bass. We would get up about five in the morning, grab a shovel, and go out in the fields to dig up worms. Laden with fishing gear and the worms, we trudged to the creek and set up on the bank. He taught me to slide the worm

When my dog, Troy, got too big for our home on Cherry Street, Uncle Walter seemed happy to give him a fine home at his farm.

over the hook head-first but let half of it loose to wiggle, since bass like live bait. Sure enough, a bass would take a bite and I'd hook him. We caught several bass that first morning—I was so proud—and headed back to the farmhouse to have fish for breakfast. When we got back to the house, I discovered that George also intended to teach me how to clean them. Do you know that fish never close their eyes? Try cutting the head off a fish who seems to be looking at you. That wasn't very pleasant, but the fried fish breakfast was delicious.

We had a blast that week flying kites, launching model gliders, learning to pilot a canoe...and the list goes on. Beside photography, I learned to target shoot with George's 22 Hornet Model 70 Winchester rifle—George was a great shot! After target practice, we reloaded the cartridges on a loading press in his hobby room over Aunt Alta's kitchen.

George also introduced me to radio-building. As I mentioned before, I loved stories and had listened to radio storytellers most of my life. George was able to show me how a radio worked, which fascinated me. We started with a crystal set, a very simple type of radio. It was fun to find a couple of Philadelphia stations by placing the "cat whisker" on different places on the crystal (it looked like a piece of coal). Then we worked with the vacuum tube radio.

As I look back on that summer, I realize how exceedingly fortunate we were to do so many fun activities—even though it was 1936, the middle of the Great Depression. George's family had resources for these pleasures even then.

This special summer week with George laid the groundwork for more wonderful visits in the coming years. Little did I realize at the time the profound impact of his lessons on my entire life.

Chapter 3

The Upper Grades

I survived elementary school and moved on to junior high.

Following my sister Josie's musical example, I began playing the mellophonium (also known as a mellophone). It looks like a simple version of a French horn but plays like a trumpet. Mr. Granger, an instrumental teacher, came to our house once a week to give me lessons on the rented school instrument I was assigned. After a year of marching in the school band with the mellophone, I moved up to trumpeter.

As seventh grade ended, I looked forward to another summer week with my older cousin George. Although I expected additional lessons in photography, I had no idea the summer would also contain information about girls. And little did I realize what was in store in eighth grade and beyond.

I took pride in playing the mellophone as a uniformed member of the Upper Moreland Marching Band.

Another Summer with George

As anticipated, the summer of 1937 brought further photographic instruction from George, beginning with how to take good pictures with a dollar box camera.

I can still hear his voice giving me advice as we tramped around the farm taking "interesting" pictures. "Make sure there's film in your camera and a well composed picture in front of you. And choose the best viewpoint. Finding a good subject to photograph is just as important as operating the camera correctly. In shooting the scene, hold the camera still and level. Support it on a table, a rock or a tripod to keep it steady while *squeezing* the shutter release."

We would then process the film and make prints in the cellar of his family's

My first camera,
a box camera,
cost one dollar
and a roll of film
was 27 cents.
(left)

My second
camera was a
Univex.
(right)

farmhouse. From the dining room, we went down a few rickety steps to the hard-packed dirt floor of the cellar. The ceiling was so low we had to sit on boxes to do most of our work, and there was no sink or running water. In the dark, George's safelight produced a dim red glow that reflected off the white-washed stone walls. With the pungent odor of chemicals came the images, appearing on our film.

When the film was washed, we would use his mom's clothes pins to attach it to clothesline strung across the cellar to dry in the stale air. Later, George would insert the negatives we made into his enlarger to project the images onto photo paper which was then processed in trays of chemicals. It was a thrill to see the images appear on paper in the red safelight.

Later that year, I made my own enlarger using a pretzel can, an old drill press stand, and an oft-borrowed lens from my sister's box camera. It worked, but the images were not very sharp. Photography quickly grew into my favorite hobby and later developed into my business and career.

During that same summer visit, George sat me down for a serious talk. He explained the differences between men and women, and how married male and female couples have babies. It was all new to me, but he made it very simple and easy to understand. It seemed logical to me and fit with everything I had heard from my buddies. As time went along, I realized that this subject was never mentioned at home, and came to believe Mom and Dad must have asked George to teach me about it for them.

Not So Pleasant Memories

Despite George's teaching, I was still very naïve about the gender topic. Returning to eighth grade that fall, I personally experienced a perversion of the subject that impacted my life forever.

It began when I started marching with the school band.

Everyone loved the way Edgar P. Headly, our music teacher, led the band. At football games, we marched precisely in straight lines, striding to certain spots on the field to spell UMHS BAND. He could play every instrument himself and enthralled the parents with his expert piano playing. He was immensely popular with almost everyone.

Mr. Headly, a bachelor, often stopped by our house to see how I was coming along with my trumpet. Mother invited him to stay for supper, and he accepted without fail. We all enjoyed his entertaining visits, and he delighted in Mother's cooking.

One evening at the dinner table, he told of a famous operetta being performed the following Friday night at The Mastbaum, a large theater in Philadelphia and asked if he could take me to see it. We would go to dinner at a hotel, see the show, and—because it would be very late—we would stop at his brother's house on the way home and stay overnight. His sister-in-law would make us a great breakfast, and we would return mid-morning Saturday.

During the Great Depression, my family could not afford to eat in restaurants or attend famous performances. So, my parents were overjoyed for me to participate in such a fine opportunity.

After school Friday, we left in Mr. Headley's shiny new Oldsmobile for Philadelphia. Mom had packed a bag for me with brand new pajamas. We had a delicious dinner at a swanky hotel and headed across the street to the theater. I loved the performance; it was first class, colorful and had great music. Afterwards, we headed to his brother's house where we were warmly greeted by his family. His brother's wife showed me my room and the bath, while the brothers talked in the living room.

I hurried to get into my new pajamas (they really smelled new). With the light turned out, I went to sleep almost immediately. The next thing I remember was being awakened by someone getting into my bed. He greeted me, and I recognized my teacher's voice. I was confused. Was he sharing my room? Was he in the wrong bed? Did I misunderstand? I sought a new sleeping position by turning away from him and wiggling to the edge of the bed. I went back to sleep.

At a later time during the night, I awoke to feel his arm under my hip. I didn't know what to think. Was he having a nightmare? I knew I wasn't. Was he sleeping? Somehow, I was able to go back to sleep.

A little later, I awoke yet again to feel his other hand on my hip. I felt sorry for him that he suffered from such nightmares, the only thing my young mind could suggest as an explanation. I fell back to sleep.

Violently awaked shortly thereafter, I felt his hands lowering my pajama bottoms. Then he was rubbing my private parts with both of his hands. I was confused and afraid. What was I to do? He retreated, removing his hands—I guess he realized I was awake. My mind continued to think this was just an awful nightmare. It was certainly that for me, although I knew I was not dreaming.

The next morning, I wanted to ask him about his nightmare. But I decided to forget about it, since he seemed so like his fine-spirited self. After a good breakfast, he dropped me off at my home, which was actually quite close.

Bewildered and very confused, I wasn't sure I could tell my mom and dad everything about the experience. I took the easy way out by just sharing the nice parts of the dinner, performance and breakfast. Mom would probably have told me I dreamt the odd part in the middle of the night.

We lived in a generation that did not talk openly about the facts-of-life or other delicate matters. Furthermore, both Mom and Dad grew up with cold, distant mothers (see Appendix B) who took little interest in their children's instruction and encouragement, which left them rather unprepared to parent Josie and me. I realize now that these reasons made it next to impossible for me to ask for their help regarding Mr. Headly.

My teacher subsequently invited me on two other outings over the next couple of years and repeated the same treatment. Confused and ill-at-ease, I often wondered who I could talk to about this delicate situation. But there was no one, so I pushed the memory to the back of my mind and committed myself to the Lord.

Probably ten years later (after the war), at a class reunion, a couple of my fellow band members told me Mr. Headly had also taken them on similar outings during our school days. One of my classmates said that his parents had recently joined others who took Headley to court. The judge declared, "You are a dirty old man. You are expelled from Pennsylvania and you shall never be allowed back in the state again."

Even when justice is served, the past cannot be reversed or erased. To this day when I open a new set of pajamas, the "new" smell reminds me of the Headly experience. And I continue to feel uneasy when using occupied public restrooms.

A Solid Foundation at Church

Life at Bethany Baptist was delightful. I sometimes sang in the choir. And Sunday nights I played trumpet in the church band. This, in a way, redeemed any bad associations I might have made between Mr. Headly the music teacher and my original — and continuing — love of music

During the summers, our evening services were held on the church lawn and neighbors would join us. Once I accepted Jesus as my Savior, I began to grow in spiritual knowledge and understanding. I loved going to church to learn, worship, and fellowship with believers.

In high school one year, I taught a Sunday school class of 12-year-old boys — what a handful! Instead of listening, I think they enjoyed putting me to the test. At that time, it was very evident to me I needed some proper training. Looking back at the canvas of my life, I see how God used this class to create in me a desire to teach, which I have done in one form or another ever since.

Mr. Lovett's Gift

During the Great Depression, some very fine gentlemen stopped at Dad's shop to sit around one of the potbelly stoves and tell stories. Mr. Lovett was one of them, and took a liking to me. One day he observed me drawing a brake for my Express Wagon. "Paul, that's a nice drawing. You should pursue that talent." How I wish he could see what I have invented and what I design today!

I am hamming it up beside
Uncle Frank Bastian,
Dad's oldest brother,
retired from the Norfolk and
Southern Railroad,
who took some of our family
by train and ferry boat
to the New York World's Fair
for a day in 1938.

The Ford pavilion at the World's Fair sported
a futuristic statue of Mercury introducing the
brand new Mercury (Ford) automobile.

George sat across the train car,
getting a kick out of me taking pictures with the
camera he taught me to use.

Taking pictures in New York
with George thrilled me! This
skyline photo was taken from
the deck of our ferry.

After the summer of 1937, Mr. Lovett discovered my photography and darkroom hobby. With great interest, he questioned me about my activities and shared with me that he too had made a few pictures in the past with developing equipment he had somewhere in his house. "I think I still have that stuff. Would you have any use for it?"

I assured him I did indeed!

He immediately took me to his beautiful nearby home. He looked through several closets before he found the darkroom items. In following him from closet to closet, room to room, we passed through Mrs. Lovett's bedroom. I remember seeing dozens and dozens of fancy glass bottles on her bureaus and around the room. Each one contained a different colored perfume. My mother had one such bottle in her bedroom. Here were so many; I was fascinated!

That day Mr. Lovett gave me a wonderful assortment of darkroom paraphernalia I could not have otherwise afforded. One item was a safelight. In the days of light-sensitive film and photo paper, this was used in a darkened room to emit a low level red light that allowed you to see a developing image. His safelight had four panels, one of which was made of ruby-red glass. A candle holder sat in the base and a chimney allowed smoke to exit at the top. I had never seen a safelight with a candle as we were well into the age of electricity. He also found trays, printing frames and other things he put into an old box and handed to me. I thanked him profusely for the treasures.

I thoroughly enjoyed Mr. Lovett's gifts. Coupled with my experiences working with George in his darkroom at the farmhouse, I was on my way to designing my first photo darkroom in the cellar of my home. Little did I know while I was working in that original darkroom on Cherry Street that later in life my photo darkroom designs would appear in many art schools, colleges and universities all over America.

On the first floor of our home, directly above my cellar darkroom was our living room and my sister's piano. Josie, a student of classical music at Beaver College with a major in voice and minor in piano, practiced many hours every day. To perfect her piano fingering, she would interrupt the song she was playing to work on a particular section...over and over and over and over again until she got it right. Frustrated by the monotony, I would eventually yell through the floor, "GO ON!" But truly, I loved hearing her play the old masters, including my favorite composer, Rachmaninoff.

And so...I received a secondary education in classical piano while enjoying my photography pursuits.

Inventions, Schemes and Side Jobs

In today's digital age, a budding photographer may run out of memory on his phone or camera, but he does not need to buy film, printing paper and chemicals like I did as a boy. My hobby required a steady source of income. During the Great Depression, jobs were scarce and some people could not even afford food.

How did I, as a kid, manage to make money to buy photo supplies during the Depression? Like my dad who had several businesses, I was an inventor with many diverse ideas, plans, and efforts—some, only a kid could have pulled off. Frankly some ideas didn't work, but many did.

A shooting gallery began my early business ventures. I owned a BB gun and a pack of 100 BBs. I decided to capitalize on my friends' desire to use my stuff. (By the way, BB has been thought to be the abbreviation for "ball bearings" but actually stands for the size of a shot, which years ago fell between B and BBB and eventually became a standard size single projectile.)

Our garage made an ideal shooting gallery, since my dad drove his car to work each day leaving it empty. I soon learned that snuffing a lighted candle was too challenging for the average target enthusiast. So, I added empty cans swinging on strings attached to a long string pulled from the front of the garage where shooters sat on boxes and rested their elbows on a wide plank.

In the beginning the gallery was a dangerous place. BBs bounced off the back wooden wall of the garage and sometimes hit customers. Determined to make this venture work — safely — I asked Mom for an old white sheet to hang between the back wall and the targets. BBs pierced the target and material, ricocheted off the wall, and hit the sheet again (not the customers), then dropped to the floor.

In between customers, I collected the used BBs at the base of the sheet. This practical discipline resulted in a perfect business plan with no overhead. I reused the BBs again and again.

To shoot at my gallery cost the customer one cent for every six BBs. No prize was awarded for hitting the cans; but if you could extinguish a lighted candle, you were awarded six extra BBs free of charge.

Word-of-mouth brought customers from all over the neighborhood — young and the young-at-heart, little shooters and big shooters, to test their skill.

Some gallery customers complained that snuffing out the candles was impossible. I would then put on a demonstration of skill as I extinguished a candle with one perfect shot. (I didn't tell them the BB must drown the wick in the soft candle wax in order to put out the flame. That was my trade secret!)

Business boomed and I soon earned the first dollar that went toward the capital investment of a second BB gun, which doubled my business. And we never ran out of "bullets."

This was a slow but sure way to make money for photo supplies. And finally, I saved enough for a significant purchase. George met me in Philadelphia to shop for my first (used) professional camera. We found just the right one, a Kodak Recomar 9x12cm Camera with six sheet film holders. I walked out of that store feeling like a big-time photographer.

This Buck Jones BB gun and single shot BB gun were the whole of my assets for my shooting gallery business.

A later business venture was a newspaper route in a wealthy neighborhood. I had 67 customers who received the *Philadelphia Evening Bulletin* six days a week. Delivering papers increased my income much faster than the shooting gallery where I was at the mercy of however many customers showed up each day. Newspaper delivery was steady work with steady pay. I looked forward to collections on Saturday. The cost for six daily papers was eighteen cents. Even during the Great Depression, some of my customers would give me two dimes or even a quarter and say, "Keep the change." At Christmas one year, an older man gave me a half-dollar. Wow!

For a short time, I worked for our janitor, Mr. Davis. I swept the floors after school each day in the fourth, fifth and sixth grade rooms. To simplify and speed-up the job, I learned to shoot the push-broom under several desks in one stroke. But Mr. Davis caught up with me and showed me that my faster method wasn't picking up all the dirt under the desks. He insisted I use the broom the correct way to do a good job. He was such a nice old man (even though I didn't care for the smell of the Apple Jack tobacco he constantly chewed).

One summer I worked at the Willow Grove Amusement Park as a soda jerk. I learned how to scoop ice cream, make milkshakes and put together great sandwiches. My stingy boss made me scoop hollow balls of ice cream for customer cones, but ones for him had to be solid. Although I felt bad for customers, I had to obey the boss. For the most part, I enjoyed the job. For a twelve-hour day, I only made two-dollars, but the perks were good—all the ice cream, milk shakes and sandwiches I could consume.

The quality of my picture-taking and darkroom skills steadily improved. By the time I was in high school (post-Depression), I was paid as much as 25 to 50 cents for my photos by various individuals.

Three o'clock one morning, Moyers Lumber Yard caught fire. Since they were located less than a block away from our house, we could feel the terrific heat while standing on our front lawn watching the blaze. I quickly got my camera and snapped a few shots. Then I phoned the editor of our local newspaper, told him I had captured the fire on film, and asked if he was going to send anyone out to cover the story.

He couldn't shake loose a photographer until later in the day and said I should send my film to him by train. He would use my pictures and have a reporter get the story by phone. That evening one of my shots appeared on the front page of the *Philadelphia Evening Bulletin*, and more of my pictures were printed in later editions of the paper.

The editor returned my film holders along with a check for fifteen dollars. That was nice money, about half the price of a good used professional camera. I was sure I was on my way to becoming a famous photographer.

A side benefit of the Moyer Lumber Yard fire was salvaged materials. I asked Mr. Moyer if I could take some of the charred tongue-and-groove wooden fence boards for a building project in my backyard. He immediately agreed and I thanked him, adding how sorry I was for his loss.

My buddies and I hauled the wood to my house and began building our newest and best bunkhouse. We turned the charred side of each board to the outside, keeping the like-new side as the inside finish. I convinced Mom that with the "new" boards we could really use some new nails, and I needed another nickel from her secret stash than never seemed to run out.

My famous picture of the Moyer's Lumberyard fire appeared on the front page
of the *Philadelphia Evening Bulletin*.

The black outer appearance of the little house didn't please everyone in the neighborhood, but we thought its rustic appearance blended well with the trees around it. This bunk was a masterpiece — but the roof still leaked. If only Mr. Gibson would make good on his offer of tarpaper (see Chapter 1).

Also during high school, I got a job as a photographer and sports writer with the *Willow Grove Guide*, our little weekly hometown paper. I also worked for our school paper, the *Willow Bark*. I reported mostly on the Upper Moreland Golden Bears football, basketball and baseball games. The editor of the *Willow Grove Guide* paid me five cents for each column inch I turned in, but she most often cut my submission short in order to "fit the space" (and her budget). She liked to run my pictures of the games — but come to think of it, she never paid me for photos. Still, I was happy to see them in print and knew it made my reporting more interesting.

The summer before my senior year of high school, I worked for the Montgomery County surveyor. He and I walked many of the country roads around Willow Grove, measuring their length and width, as well as noting their condition. The surveyor took the lead and carried the steel tape. He marked the road with chalk, walked ahead about 100 feet while I held my end of the tape on his mark, and made notes as he worked his way forward. This job was valuable educationally and financially; it paid me 25 cents an hour. Now that was good money! I asked many questions, and the surveyor graciously answered each one. Later my math teacher taught us surveying as related to trigonometry (one

ℝOVE GUID

rise — **Home Advertising**

WEDNESDAY, APRIL 2, 1941

Upper Moreland Junior High Champs
Of the Montgomery County League

Photo by Paul Sebastian
Left to right: First Row—George Roberts, Stewart Webster, Walter Howell, Roy Nuss, Joe Betzle. Second Row—Henry Weinberger Martin Weinberger, Frank Summeril, Carl Swayze, Lloyd Clifford. Third Row—Frank Clifford, Coach Dunn, Harry Leven.

By Paul Sebastian

Shores Named Chiefs Ass'n. Head

Upper Moreland Twp. Police Chief Succeeds Chief Bertz of Royersford

PROMINENT SPEAKERS

Proper training of the policeman was stressed last Wednesday night by John F. Sears, special agent in charge of the Philadel...

The Upper Moreland Junior High tied with Whitpain for the Montco League cup until Tuesday, March 18. Upper Moreland and Whitpain then fought for the victory which Upper Moreland won. This game was played on Abington's floor. The final score was 16 to 15 in Upper Moreland's favor. The boys really worked hard for this cup and they well deserve it.

The boys owe a lot to Mr. Dunn, mathematics instructor at Upper Moreland, for his fine assistance in coaching that enabled them to win the Montco League Cup.

Some of the winning scores from the Junior High schedule were: Collegeville 36-9, Hatfield 14-4, Low- (Continued on Page 3)

After two years of sports writing and photography, I finally earned a byline for my text and pictures in the *Willow Grove Guide* (left).

of my favorite subjects). My summer surveying experience made that math lesson come alive for me.

Even with all these jobs and others, I constantly struggled to acquire enough money to buy film, paper and chemicals. Sheet film for my new camera was very expensive, so I tried to make every shot count.

High School Classes

I received excellent grades in mathematics and enjoyed those classes most. My high school math teacher, Mr. Mathias, was a civil engineer. Because of the Great Depression, he could not get an engineering job, so he applied and was accepted to teach at my school. A very orderly person who used the blackboards profusely, he lettered every word and figure carefully, drawing very straight lines, and he made math practical and meaningful for his students.

Even after school he worked on projects that would help us learn. One time he used the school shop to make a five-foot-long facsimile of an engineer's slide rule and mounted it atop his classroom's blackboard. He was tall and could easily reach it, showing us how to employ a slide rule for calculating. Then, from the dime store in Willow Grove, he purchased a 25-cent slide rule for each student. As he adjusted the big slide rule at the front of the room, we followed him with our regular-sized slide rules, quickly learning how to calculate.

Later, he utilized wood from several out-of-commission school desks stored in the school to make transits to teach us surveying techniques. A transit is a calibrated telescope used to determine horizontal and vertical angles when surveying the boundaries of a plot of land. He mounted dime store protractors on his homemade transits to teach us how to calculate angles.

He used his free time to lay out traverses in the athletic field that gave us opportunity to try real-life surveying. In teams of three, students measured and recorded angles with our transits, and then returned to the classroom to lay out our

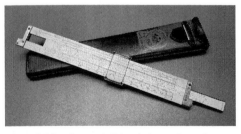

I used this advanced sliderule in my Penn State engineering studies, years after Mr. Mathias introduced a simple version to our math class.

fieldwork on paper, aided by the protractors. If our measurements came out, we were awarded an A+ for excellent field and drawing board work. This particular lesson resonated with me as I reflected back on my experiences working for the county surveyor. Mathematics was alive and understood in Mr. Mathias' classes, and I loved it.

I said to him one day, "I wish I could letter like you do."

He said, "Oh, you can! You just have to keep practicing."

Years later I discovered he was right. Mr. Mathias' diligent efforts on behalf of his students greatly impacted my life and my later career in engineering.

You may remember that my Aunt Alta seemed to favor me, even as a young child. When I got to high school, she championed one of my school projects. Mr. Graves our shop teacher showed us a brightly-painted miniature birdhouse with a little red bird perched in front. It was supported with a wire bracket you could stick in a flowerpot or put in your garden. Mr. Graves said we needed a new table saw in the shop and could raise money for it by making and selling birdhouses. He set up a production line so kids could assemble the birdhouses and paint them after school. Everyone sold birdhouses for 15 cents each. Aunt Alta bought 35 from me and distributed them to the ladies in her Bible class, making me one of the top salesmen.

Miss Barnhart taught art, and I found her classes fascinating. My early attitude toward reading art books was sadly mistaken. I had originally thought: why should I spend time reading about others' art when I can create my own? But the more I learned, the more I realized the value of study and reading. As creative as I was, I knew I had to find out more. I believe it was this understanding, first in art class, that began developing my love of learning—

This recent picture shows the transit I used many years ago to survey the campus of Lancaster Bible College.

and reading to learn. Miss Barnhart helped me appreciate the art of the masters *while* encouraging me with my own artwork. I advanced rapidly and looked forward to every session.

As a senior, I was chosen with two others from my class to participate in a program offered by Beaver College, the girl's school where my sister Josie had studied music. Our high school was invited to send three or four students (girls or boys) for two hours per week of instruction in basic art at no charge.

Every Thursday we were transported to the college where we received exceptional training with individual attention. I was enthralled to see the college students at work on different projects. I recall watching with fascination as one student painted a silk ribbon over a beautiful basket of fruit. The smooth skin of an apple in that basket looked so real I found it hard to believe I was looking at oils on canvas. I didn't attempt anything that difficult because I was surely a novice — but it amazed and motivated me.

One of the professors in our program asked us to create a sketch from a model repeatedly walking around the room as well as ascending and descending the steps of a small platform. "Select and freeze in your minds a certain body position, then sketch it on paper," the teacher told us. Although we were required to bring a large pad of sketch paper and pencil, for some reason I took a ball pen and a bottle of India ink instead of the pencil. My blunder pleased my professor because by using pen and ink rather than a pencil, I was unable to erase any lines; I had to get it right on the first try. It is next to impossible to render a reasonable replica of a person who never stops moving. But I loved the challenge and had great fun. The professor's positive comments still echo in my memory today.

Josie's Education and Graduation

I mentioned previously that my sister Josie attended Beaver College. Where I was talented with drawing and photography, she was more interested and gifted in music. And she was very smart, receiving straight A's throughout her entire education.

Even so, at her high school graduation in 1933, it surprised everyone that Josie was presented with a full four-year scholarship to Beaver College, for in those days such a thing was unheard of at Upper Moreland High School. And remember that this was during the Depression! It was quite welcome in our home. We were certainly not poor, but we were not wealthy like most of the girls who attended Beaver.

Josie was a poor girl who attended a rich girls' private school. Having talent and/or good grades were not prerequisites for attending Beaver College; perspective students needed only money and status. Most of the girls came from extremely wealthy families; some even had their own car in an era when families had one car for everyone or none at all. The college experience for these girls was almost like a four-year vacation at a resort. In a real sense though, it was a safe place where they were closely monitored and mentored in the fine arts and social graces.

Josie possessed a beautiful singing voice, had developed fabulous piano playing skill, and always earned top grades. Her stunning natural talent often gave her the lead solo in special presentations at Beaver. But Josie stood apart, because Mom made her dresses and packed her lunches. She lived at home and took the trolley to college every day, carrying her books and her lunch in a brown paper bag.

It pains me to think of the humiliation she must have felt and the possible taunting or snubs from some of the well-to-do girls in her class. She had a few close classmates but very little social life with them. Inviting any of them to her home on Cherry Street was out of the question.

As Josie's graduation from Beaver College grew near, Aunt Alta thought about a special gift for Josie. She talked to our Mom about what would be most appropriate and meaningful. They listed several things, but one idea surpassed the rest — a Saturday afternoon tea at the farmhouse with Josie's classmates and professors.

A tea at Aunt Alta's would be so fitting, especially when compared to one at Cherry Street! Aunt Alta knew how to plan such affairs down to the tiniest detail, from distributing printed invitations to the correct pouring of tea. And my family was so very grateful that Uncle Walter and Aunt Alta had the money to throw a party like this during the Great Depression, for we certainly did not.

Josie was amazed and very pleased when every girl in her class told her they would attend, and even some of the professors. I think her classmates liked her much more than she ever realized.

The Lord gave us a picture-perfect Saturday afternoon a week before the graduation. We arrived at Aunt Alta's some time before noon that day. As we drove down the farmhouse lane, we noticed the outbuildings and grounds sparkling, nothing out of place. It looked most inviting. Dad didn't stay; he "had work to do and teas were meant for ladies."

Aunt Alta warmly greeted Mother, Josie and me and told us everything was going as planned and would be ready by the time the guests arrived. She also informed us that George had contracted the flu and was sick in bed. She encouraged me to look in on him and say hello. All these pretty girls coming to his house and he gets sick. Poor George!

Inside were several young girls I had never seen before, dressed alike in black dresses with little white aprons, white stockings and black shoes. Going up to greet George in his

My sweet sister Josie graduated at the top of her class from Beaver Girls' School.

bedroom, I saw more of these girls upstairs too. Looking out the windows I observed a number of young men in black suits gathering outside. I learned later in the day that they were from Aunt Alta's church, hired to help guests park and escorting them to the house. This was going to be some event!

George asked me to keep him informed since he was so sick he couldn't leave his room. So, as things happened I reported to George. I was all around, seen but not heard.

I learned later that Aunt Alta trained the girls, upstairs and downstairs, in how to conduct themselves in every detail; and that was very evident.

Looking up the farm lane I spotted the first car approaching, and others following. The young fellows on duty outside were ready and in position. The cars looked shiny and new; some were convertibles. Each of Josie's classmates wore fancy dresses, and several even had escorts. As they entered the living room they deposited their social cards in a large polished brass dish and were warmly greeted by Josie as she introduced Mom, Aunt Alta and Miss. Standish. The downstairs and upstairs girls led them through the old farmhouse while other guests arrived. Everyone was captivated by the old renovated farmhouse which had not lost its character or charm with its walk-in fireplace, quaint kitchen and the list goes on and on. A few of Josie's professors came to the tea and she was so delighted that they did.

Teaching during the war, Josie directed the Upper Moreland High School marching band.

As I observed the guests arriving and enjoying themselves thoroughly, I reported every detail to George. He ate it up, happy for Josie as we all were. I described how Aunt Alta poured tea for everyone as the girls nibbled on tiny sandwiches and delicious little cakes. I figured I had better wait, then relished a generous sampling after the guests went home.

This turned out to be an even more meaningful graduation gift than had been anticipated. Aunt Alta was so pleased with everything that day (except poor George's predicament).

As part of Josie's graduation requirement, each music student had to compose an original piece and perform it in a formal setting. Josie composed an obbligato to be sung with a choir to "Angels from the Realms of Glory." At her graduation, Beaver's Class of '37 marched into the auditorium dressed in their black caps and gowns, holding lighted candles and singing "Angels from the Realms of Glory," while Josie sang her beautiful obbligato. It was a very moving experience. Of course, I knew it well; that is, I had heard it practiced many, many times at home.

Josie received a Bachelor of Music degree with honors that day, but since she wanted to be a music teacher, she went on to the University of Pennsylvania to be certified. Several years later, after I had graduated, she filled a long-term substitute position at our school while the music teacher served in the US Army. I was so proud of my sister.

My Graduation and Choices for Further Education

My own graduation from Upper Moreland High School in 1941 was rather uneventful when compared with Josie's graduation eight years earlier. She had graduated amid fanfare from winning the scholarship, while I was just glad to be done with school!

My family, relatives and many of my friends advised me to go on to college. No, I had more than enough of school. However — within a week after graduation — Mom found an ad in the Philadelphia newspaper offering a 400-hour defense course in engineering drafting at the Mastbaum Vocational School in the Kensington area of Philadelphia. It was free, paid for by Uncle Sam.

World War II had begun during my junior year of high school; however, my life was impacted only by the rising economy due to more plentiful job opportunities. At the time I was considering the Mastbaum course, it did not occur to me that the government was offering it as an incentive to raise up engineers for the war effort.

I just knew this relatively short engineering course would appease family and friends without committing me to years of more schooling. I loved to draw, so I signed up. Later I would look back and clearly see God's leading in this excellent decision.

Three months of eight-hour days, under the tutelage of Mr. Gabler, turned me into a pretty good mechanical draftsman. In addition to teaching easy-to-understand lessons from Frenches' classic textbook on Drafting, Mr. Gabler thoroughly answered my many questions and encouraged me in every way possible.

The next step was an engineering job.

Mother's older sister, my Aunt Lillie was married to Armon Greul. Uncle Armon was a mechanical engineer who worked in Wilmington, Delaware for the du Pont Company. He was always interested in my projects through the years. Knowing that I was looking for a job, he asked me if I'd liked to work for du Pont in their engineering department. I immediately jumped at the possibility. Sure enough, he got me the job.

Every day I traveled from Willow Grove to Wilmington. The two-and-a-half-hour commute each way by public conveyance cost me about half my pay, which started at 40 cents an hour. At first I delivered blueprints to three floors of architects and engineers. Were my eyes ever opened to design and power plant operations! As I got to know some of the engineers, I would linger at their work areas to ask questions and look at their very complicated drawings. This furthered my education, but it still wasn't enough.

Within ten months, I had received two raises. I now sat at my own work area complete with drawing board and exciting projects — making a measly

56 cents per hour. One day I said to the personnel manager, Mr. Bergen, "What can I do to receive better pay?"

"Paul, this is the way it is. You go out and get 35 years of engineering experience real quick, or you can go to college and study engineering."

I was once again facing the advice my family and friends had given me after high school. I could not argue with inevitability. I needed more education.

Penn State offered the best four-year course in mechanical engineering for miles around. I had considered architecture — my primary interest since the days of building bunks — as my major. But my dad dissuaded me. "Son, someday you might be called upon to design a hotel with a bar…or something worse. I don't want you put in that situation." So, I had promised him I would take mechanical engineering. I discovered later it was heavy in steam power plant design and very light in machine design. But later yet, I looked back and saw how God was weaving a master plan that encompassed every decision.

Dad and I didn't know this at the time, but I would stick with the program until I was called up to active duty in World War II a year later. I was at a crossroad and about to see God's working in my life while experientially learning the truth of Romans 8:28 and 29: "And we know that all things work together for good to those who love God, to those who are the called according to His purpose. For whom He foreknew, He also predestined to be conformed to the image of His Son, that He might be the firstborn among many brethren."

I looked forward to Penn State with a mixture of hopeful anticipation and that same feeling of dread I had experienced on the first morning of first grade.

Chapter 4

College, World War II and Missions

The year between high school graduation and entering college had been filled with the Mastbaum course and ten months of work at duPont. In September of 1942, I became a freshman at Penn State College in the School of Engineering.

The room I rented at Mrs. Richell's house did not include board, so I took my meals at Mrs. Matill's. Many ladies in the bustling town of State College opened their homes to students who did not care to live in one of the campus dormitories. I did not personally know anyone at Penn State or desire a roommate, so I chose to room downtown.

Meals at Mrs. Matill's were a far cry from Aunt Alta's posh feasts. When I reached Mrs. Matill's each morning for breakfast, bowls were already filled with cereal. One day, as I poured milk into my bowl, three roaches scurried out from under the bran flakes. Ah, the adventures of a poor college student.

Maybe that kitchen wouldn't pass today's health inspections, but Mrs. Matill had a heart of gold, and I can still picture old Mr. Matill rocking on the front porch. I didn't know until much later that my future wife moved into the Matills' boarding house the following year.

A pleasant surprise awaited me during the first few days of my college experience. When a professor examined samples of drawings and lettering I had brought from home, he exempted me from his introductory drawing course. And my other classes progressed with more ease than I had anticipated.

My personality made me unassuming, quiet, introspective and creative. I did not seek out activities on campus, not being all that adventuresome by nature. Although I slowly developed friends in some of my classes, my social life took a backseat to studies. I was also a year older than many of the other incoming freshmen.

Due to my sister's musical pursuits, classical music and piano playing filled my childhood and resulted in a great love for the music of the masters. December 1942, Sergei Rachmaninoff came to Penn State to perform. I was lucky to get a ticket and enjoy his concert; he died a few months later. The downside of that event—and my whole first year—was having no one with whom I could share special moments.

Freshmen PE Class

I played baseball in high school but quickly found my skills sorely lacking as I watched the Penn State team hit the ball during the first practice of my freshmen year. I decided then that I should stick to engineering. However, all students were required to take physical education (PE) classes where we were exposed to various sports, exercises and healthful activities.

I will never forget one particular class. The boxing coach walked up to our group and struck fear in those of us who recognized him as Leo Hauck, the famous prize fighter from Lancaster, Pennsylvania. I had seen his wins written up in a Philadelphia newspaper.

Leo Hauck, born in 1888 in Lancaster, began boxing in 1902 as a flyweight. He successfully fought in every weight division up to heavyweight. After his death in 1950, Hauck was inducted into the Ring Magazine hall of fame (1969), the Pennsylvania Sports Hall of Fame (1972), and enshrined within the International Boxing Hall of Fame (2012). His nickname was the Lancaster Thunderbolt.

Standing fear-stricken in that freshmen PE class, I beheld this famous prize fighter with his flattened nose and cauliflower ears (traits of a boxer) and his bushy eyebrows. Quaking in my sneakers, I began inconspicuously working my way to the back of the student group. He spoke to us in rather broken English, standing there in his boxing shorts and gloves. Then he looked at me in the back, pointed the big thumb of his mitt in my direction and said, "You. Come out here." My heart stopped and I tried to ignore him. But he called again, "You there," and waved me out to the front of the group. Then he urged me to hit him by tapping the thumb of his mitt on his nose. He kept it up, but I knew if I did I would end up on the gym floor. Thankful, he gave up, rejecting me for a more agreeable student. Whew! That's the closest I ever wanted to come to a boxing career.

Enlistment in World War II

By the time I was a freshman at Penn State, our country had been embroiled

Through a dirty train window, I waved at Ma, Josie and Dad as I departed for the army.

in World War II for three years. However, on the campus I was far more aware of it than I had been at home. Among other studies, I enrolled in an ROTC (Reserve Officers Training Corps) class.

One day during our ROTC class, we were told that every student who volunteered for active duty that day would be permitted to finish their four-year program at Penn State before being called into active service. With an offer like that, all my classmates and I enlisted.

Despite the promise, immediately after our freshmen year, we were placed into active duty at the Fort George Mead induction center in Denton, Maryland. I was shocked—we all were! How could they do this to us? It soon became obvious our military needed more and more men as the war effort escalated on both the Pacific and European fronts.

On May 27, 1943, at age 19, I boarded a train at Philadelphia's Broad Street Station bound for Fort Mead. I can remember almost crying as I looked through my train window at Mother, Dad and Josie, waving goodbye to me as my train pulled away from the station. It could have been my last farewell; but for the grace of God, I survived the war with only malaria fever.

At Fort Mead I was interviewed by an officer who was perfectly fitted for his work. He knew just what to ask each enlistee. I reached this conclusion due to his strategic line of questioning. Since my mother did not want me to be a pursuit (fighter) pilot (my first choice), I told the officer about my skills and accomplishments in photography (my second choice). I loved photography and thought I could shoot movies of the war as seen in newsreels, or take the kind of amazing shots I had seen in *LIFE* magazine that would enhance people's understanding of the war in Europe and the Pacific Islands.

But my efforts to convince the man of my invaluable skills were in vain, as I learned the following day I was shipping out to Fort Belvoir, Virginia where I would join the Corps of Engineers.

Army engineers built roads, bridges and buildings; and they strategically blew up bridges in combat zones—just to name a few of their activities during World War II. I suppose my high school art and math grades, the concentrated defense course at Mastbaum where I learned engineering drawing, my ten months with the duPont Company, and my first year at Penn State in mechanical engineering with ROTC training outweighed my pitch to be a combat photographer with the Signal Corps. But truly, I'm certain it was the loving hand of God that guided and protected me through His plan for my life and service for Him. I am reminded of Proverbs 16:9, "A man's heart plans his way, but the Lord directs his steps."

Fort Belvoir

I was placed in a 22-week combat engineer basic training class headed to England for the D-Day invasion of France. I wasn't happy about facing five and a half months of this kind of training and living, but I had no other choice. This prospect required me to fully trust my Lord to continue directing my steps.

Fort Belvoir contained rows and rows of temporary wooden barracks that had been quickly constructed to house all the recruits learning combat engineering. Lack of privacy was a part of war I never got used to. I lived in a

At 19 (left) I began the demanding 22-week army combat course.

barracks that housed 60 some men on two floors, with large open shower/toilet rooms. In addition to little personal space, we were unable to make plans for the next day, the next month, maybe the next year...and maybe forever. Discipline was very strict. I took great comfort in reading the Scriptures and pouring out my heart to God. I wondered what my comrades did to ease their tension. Most of them didn't seem to have any knowledge of God.

The training at Fort Belvoir was rigorous to say the least. The bugle sounded reveille at 5AM, beginning a flurry of preparation that culminated in a rollcall formation at six. We then marched to the mess hall for breakfast and marched back again to the barracks to make beds and straighten our foot lockers. Then we fell into formation with our rifles, piled into trucks and rode off to practice at the shooting range. Back to the barracks a little later, we would get ready for lunch and march to the mess hall—sometimes singing or counting aloud our cadence, "Left... Left... I had a good wife but she Left... Left... Left..." with the left foot hitting the ground at each "Left."

In the afternoons, we were trucked to the demolition area far away at the end of camp where our platoon sergeant, assisted by the corporal, demonstrated how to handle explosives and how to set dynamite charges to blow up bridges, railroad tracks and other important targets. After the evening meal at the mess hall, we had an hour or two of free time before lights-out at nine. Every day was the same routine except for different lessons.

Once on a camping excursion, we set up a field kitchen with water supply, dug a slip trench toilet facility and slept in pup tents. My half of the tent connected with my buddy's half and kept the two of us rather dry, except for the night we endured a downpour. Several days of this trip were spent on an obstacle course that I was sure was designed by a crazy person.

On the second Friday of my 22-week training course, at eight in the evening, my company was scheduled for a 25-mile forced march with full pack. Some time that afternoon, one of my buddies said, "Hey, Sebastian, you'd better check the bulletin board at the Orderly Room. You're shipping out."

Wow! I immediately checked and found he was right. I was going somewhere at four o'clock, but where?

The Next Assignment

I packed my barracks bag and was ready at four. An army truck pulled up on time and I was told to get in. The military rarely tells an enlisted man where he is going; no information at all. I didn't know what to think being singled out like that. I bounced along in the truck for a very short time, and then we stopped.

"This is it, Sebastian," the driver told me.

As the vehicle rumbled off, I took in my surroundings and immediately realized I was still at Fort Belvoir but now at the old permanent base. The beautiful colonial brick buildings gave way to shade trees and green fields. This was quite a change from the other side of Belvoir.

I soon learned I was enrolled in a twelve-week engineering, drawing and map making training course. Trading that initial 22-week combat training course for this new course of study I truly loved was not only an escape from a miserable life but a very gracious gift of God and answer to my prayers.

A buddy took this posed picture along the Potomac River at Fort Belvoir.

My class was comprised of 94 GIs (GI stands for "government issue" — although to be honest, I'm not sure how that came to mean "soldier"). I reveled in my studies and the work. I spent many extra hours on my drawings trying for perfection.

Just two weeks after I began this new course, I was called to Captain Hammond's office. We exchanged salutes, and he said, "Sit down, Sebastian."

I sat and wondered what he would say next.

"Your grades are the best in your class. We need another instructor. Would you like to join our cadre of instructors?" He paused and made eye contact. "Or would you like to stay with your class and go overseas?"

Easy answer. "Sir, I'd like to be an instructor." Now I paused. "But I've never taught drawing before."

He put the paperwork in front of me. "I'll assign you to an officer who will make an instructor out of you. He'll tutor you. You start immediately."

After my first classroom presentation to over a hundred GIs, I met with Lt. John Steinman. He reviewed each point on his check list, revealing that I did quite well and received a passing grade. The one failure he pointed out was lack of eye contact. I had been so afraid I would forget something that I never looked at anyone in the class the entire period. I never made that mistake again.

Lt. Steinman was a kind man who spent considerable time with me. He regularly sat in the back of my classroom and evaluated my preparation, delivery, subject knowledge, ability to correctly answer questions…and, yes, eye contact. His patient critiques helped me develop into a fine instructor — for

Many students were enrolled in my map-making course.

the army and for a future only God could see at this point.

One of my more memorable teaching experiences began the day I was given an experimental class of 50 WACs (members of the Women's Army Corps). I was nineteen and ill-prepared to deal with feminine emotions, from giggling to crying. Most of the women had little to no interest and/or ability in engineering drawing. And the absentee rate was unusually high. The commanding officers realized the experiment was a failure and shut it down by the sixth week. Only four WACs made the grade, stayed the course and graduated.

I fondly recall one of my WAC students. Dorcas was a professional sculpture artist. She invited me to join her and her WAC companion to visit in the Washington, D.C. home of a wealthy woman who had commissioned Dorcas to sculpt her. A multicourse dinner was served by a butler, beginning with fruit juice. A personal finger bowl sat at each place setting, confounding me until Dorcas gestured to show me how to cleanse my fingers between courses. I was so awestruck by the details of the dinner, I don't remember the food. I do recall that the meal ended with a delicious dessert and coffee, after which we retired to the living room where Dorcas arranged lighting, positioned our hostess, and proceeded with her sculpting. I enthusiastically watched her shape the half-size clay model she had worked on during previous visits. The hostess was exceedingly pleased by Dorcas' work, and I was thrilled to be a part of the observers. As the army chauffeur took us back to Fort Belvoir, Dorcas asked to do a small sculpture of me. I still have the plaster cast she completed a few weeks later.

As I recount this memory, I am connecting Dorcas' sculpting with my own adventures in clay. Having retrieved her bust of my young self from my basement memory room, I now notice details I did not appreciate as much before my own sculpting experiences (*see the end of Chapter 6, "Playing with Clay"*). And I am fascinated again by the intricate details of God's plans for His children.

Thanks to Lt. Steinman's mentoring, I successfully taught hundreds of GIs how to make engineering drawings during my 13 months as an instructor at Fort Belvoir. He and I became great friends. In fact, he told me to look him up after the war if I wanted to work with him in his Wisconsin lumber business.

Dorcas sculpted this likeness of me.
Photo Credit: Keith Baum

While I was teaching at Fort Belvoir, the army announced a rotation program that gave

Of the 50 WACs who took my drawing course (upper photo; sculptress Dorcas is the second row from the top, second from the left), only four graduated along with these men (lower photo), standing here in front of one of Fort Belvoir's beautiful permanent buildings, so unlike the plentiful temporary wooden structures used during basic training.

Enjoying a rare pass, I delighted my mom, sister and dad with a 3-day home visit
during my teaching days at Fort Belvoir.

anyone who served overseas for 22 months or longer an offer to rotate with someone who had not. Shortly thereafter, I received word of my trade and faced an overseas assignment in Europe or the Pacific. Thanking my Lord for the great opportunity I'd had to teach a subject I loved so well, I now had a new opportunity to trust Him — come what may.

Waiting at Fort Belvoir for deployment, I spent several fascinating days observing a Hollywood camera crew shoot a training film on how to operate a Galleon Grader (a heavy-duty earth scrapper used to carve a road through a jungle or clear land for an airport runway). The crew was very friendly and gave me short ends of unexposed 35mm film that were enough to last me through the end of the war. (Today, I look back and marvel at God's timing and provision in things like this waiting period, where at the time I did not realize he was equipping me to take pictures throughout the war.)

Sent Overseas

On Christmas Day 1944, I left Fort Indiantown Gap on a train, having received an order to depart from the Port of Embarkation in Long Beach, California. About five days later, I reached California and boarded a Kaiser troopship with 5,800 other GIs, plus lots of marines and sailors, and headed to the Southwest Pacific.

I turned 20 aboard ship on January 4. No celebration ensued.

While on the ocean, I spent hours designing and drawing buildings. As the days passed, I found a couple GIs who were architects in civilian life. They graciously critiqued my sketches and showed me perspective and rendering techniques. I so appreciated their willingness to help me learn and better my drawing skills. This helped pass the monotonous days of nothing but waves, sky and fellow comrades.

Day by day we zigzagged our way across the Pacific Ocean, through waters infested with Japanese submarines, until at last we reached port at Melbourne, Australia. We took on needed supplies but were not allowed to disembark. Imagine the ship filled with almost 6,000 young men who had not had any fun in a good number of days—we would surely have torn up that quaint and lovely little town.

Leaving the port of Melbourne, we were not, as usual, told the next destination, though we could ascertain by the position of the sun that we were headed west.

After 44 days on the boat, extremely close quarters and a very limited menu, we finally docked in Calcutta, India. What a strange place with very unusual sights and strong odors! It seemed like I was watching an issue of the *National Geographic Magazine* come to life. This was not a movie scene or dream sequence; it was real. For days, still not allowed to disembark, we watched a strange drama as the Ganges River flowed into the Bay of Bengal with every person and animal using the water for every imaginable task, even tending to their toilet and laundry necessities—in the "holy" water of the Ganges. Later, I learned I contracted malaria fever there in Calcutta. I learned to control it by taking Atabrine tablets each day until I reached China.

India

While teaching, I had been upgraded to the rank of Technician Fourth Grade (T-4). I had anticipated being a structural draftsman when I arrived

After serving at Fort Belvoir for a year and a half, I traveled by train to the west coast and then spent another 44 days on a ship traveling across the Pacific Ocean to Calcutta, India.

overseas; however, my first assignment in India was to supervise the transport of vehicles from Calcutta to Ledo, the west end of the Burma Road. With trepidation, I signed the manifest paperwork making me responsible for 56 new 6x6 trucks, each containing a new Jeep.

Several GIs loaded the trucks on wide-gauge railroad flatcars. But instead of leaving for our destination straight away, we had to wait a day for our steam locomotive to be serviced.

Forced to spend the night with my trucks in the freight yard, I climbed into one and tried to get comfortable. Curious noises outside made it difficult to sleep: unfamiliar music, exclamations in a language I did not understand, howling of dogs and jackals... Inside, mosquitos made me their supper. Trucks used in the jungle do not have tight cab enclosures, and I had no repellent at my disposal, so I became a mosquito feast. At one point, I illuminated my truck seat

Upon arrival in India, we pitched our tents just east of Calcutta at Camp Kanchrapara and enjoyed the "luxury" of living outside.

with a flashlight and found it black with pests. I brushed away the bugs and blood — my blood — which covered the seat. I was glad I had started taking my Atabrine the day before!

We got underway at daybreak, traveling out of Calcutta toward Ledo. Our train chugged through the lush jungle for miles and miles on the wide-gauge railroad tracks.

Arriving at the mighty Brahmaputra River, our train stopped and we unloaded the vehicles. The Brahmaputra is a wild jungle waterway, impossible to ford. So, a primitive wooden raft ferried us across, two trucks at a time. A cable from shore to shore kept the raft on course as it moved very slowly with waves washing over the deck.

In a few hours all our trucks made it safely across the river, and we reloaded the vehicles onto narrow-gauge flatcars to again head northeast through the jungle toward Assam, India's most northeast province. It was fun to wave to the village kids, throw them a coin and see them scramble to find it. When we came to the end of the second rail line, other GIs met us to unload the train, and we formed a convoy and snaked our way up and down the mountains. This time I was one of the drivers.

One night we came across an army base, a black trucking company. At this time in history, US army units were segregated. Having lost track of time in the jungle, we asked what day it was. "Easter Sunday" was the reply. Then our hosts graciously invited us into their mess hall for chow (we had been living on cold canned corn-beef-hash for quite some time). I still remember the mouth-watering aroma of the complete hot turkey dinner they served us—a meal I'll never forget. We asked how they obtained such extravagant food. One guy chuckled and admitted, "We deliver food to officer mess halls and other prominent places. If a case of this or that happens to fall off the truck …well, you get the picture."

We convoyed over steep mountains with hairpin curves to Ledo where I safely delivered all 56 trucks and Jeeps. Thinking back, I do not recall receiving a receipt for delivering all that hardware!

Finally, I reached my official appointment in Ledo at the headquarters of the 1187th Engineer Construction Group. I had been rotated into the position of chief design engineer. Starting in 1937, this construction group had built and maintained the single lane truck and tank passage over the Himalayan Mountains of Burma, from Ledo to Kunming (China).

The US flew tons of supplies to the Chinese over "the hump," the Himalayan Mountains. These are the tallest mountains in the world—so high, only our C46s with their twin 4000hp Pratt & Whitney engines were able to fly over. Heavy trucks, tanks and supplies could not be flown into China; they

A fellow GI stands in the middle of native Indian workers using their heads to carry heavy loads.

In my typical uniform, I am hunkered down at the 1187th Engineer Construction
Group Ledo in Assam, India.

were driven over a thousand miles through dense jungle on Burmese primitive
roadways.

This Ledo-Burma Road provided a backdoor supply passage for the US to
deliver military goods needed by the Chinese to defeat Japanese forces. Before
V-J (Victory over Japan) Day, the road was named The General Joseph Stilwell
Road in honor of the general under whose command the Japanese were totally
defeated in India and Burma.

I reported at headquarters and asked which tent was mine. The first
sergeant told me all the tents were occupied and I would have to erect my own.
When I asked where to obtain one, all he said was "Midnight Requisition" and
walked away. Talking with other GIs, I learned I could go to the supply tent
and take whatever I needed. Some of the fellows helped me pick out equipment
and set it up in the tent village.

I learned Japanese soldiers were just 15 miles away, but no one expected to
see them because Ledo was well fortified. Even so, knowing they were close
unsettled me. Thank God, I remained safe. Yet again, He rescued me from
combat with enemy forces.

The troops at our base in Ledo had been without a bugler for many months.
Someone looking through my service record found that I had played the
trumpet in my high school band. I was called to the orderly room, handed the
bugle and told to wake the troops each morning. My fellow servicemen none
too kindly complained about my additional assignment, not because of my
playing but because they had to get up.

For the next six months, I was more favorably known for my designs of
military structures and creative solutions for maintaining the section of the
Ledo Road under the care of my unit.

The War Ends

Lasting six years, World War II was the most widespread and deadliest war in human history. Involving more than 100 million people from over 30 countries, and depleting economic, industrial, and scientific assets, it included the Holocaust (11 million Jews annihilated) and the atomic bombings of Hiroshima and Nagasaki, and resulted in over 50-85 million military and civilian casualties.

My buddy Chuck (far left) watches a loaded pedicab, a frequent sight in India.
GIs most often traveled by Jeep.

World War II was fought on two fronts: in Europe and Africa and in the islands of the Pacific. The European war concluded with the German surrender on May 8, 1945. V-E Day, or Victory in Europe Day, was a day enshrined in history and emblazoned in my memory.

Sitting at my drawing board in the engineering office that morning, I had heard a commotion, screams of jubilation and a tremendous report of steam whistles in our nearby freight yard. Everyone in the office rushed outside to find out what was going on, overjoyed to find the war in Europe had ended. Our weekly *Yankee Magazine* gave us details within a few days: The Battle of the Bulge and the ensuing maneuvers of our forces and the allies that brought about the end.

Several thoughts stirred in my mind. *We* were still at war with Japan. As much as I wanted to go home, I knew I had to stay with my buddies and see our war here to the end.

After the surrender, my comrades and I were ushered into an outdoor theater and shown uncensored movies revealing the atrocities of the Holocaust. We had not known of the Nazi death camps and gassing facilities prior to this. I cannot put into words how I felt.

Three months later, while I was still stationed in India, the Japanese surrendered. They never used the word "surrender." Too proud to admit defeat, they said they "ceased hostilities." In my estimation, the Japanese were even more brutal than the Germans, based on my knowledge of their prisoner torture, death camps and Kamikaze activity. I cannot imagine any human being doing what they did. Regardless, August 15, 1945 became V-J Day, or Victory Over Japan Day.

I was elated that the war was finally over. I was ready to go home. But that was not to be.

Post War Clean Up in China

My next destination was to be Shanghai, China. I had a thrilling flight in a C-46 transport plane from nearby Chabua, over the hump of snow-covered Himalayan Mountains (Burma) and into Kunming. We flew on to Canton and then into Shanghai, a busy international city trying to recover from the Japanese occupation.

Re-assigned — with the new rank Master Sergeant — to the 100th Quartermaster American Graves Registration Group in Shanghai, my work was to send out teams of men with equipment and with a Chinese interpreter to find the remains of our fallen comrades and give them a military funeral in Shanghai.

Almost daily we received letters from magistrates all over China offering to lead us to the remains of our Air Force and Flying Tigers airmen, casualties the Chinese had hidden from the Japanese during the war. After repeatedly sending men out on these retrieval expeditions, I developed a desire to accompany them to share what they witnessed.

Finally my opportunity arrived. A report came in from Pudong, just east of Shanghai. Our interpreter translated the message: a magistrate knew of a US B-24 bomber, converted into a

These all-wise Chinese soothsayers were a common sight on many Shanghai sidewalks.

A typical scene showing the thousands who thronged the Shanghai streets.

gasoline tank transport, that had been hit by Japanese tracer fire and exploded in midair. This story checked out with our Air Force records. The letter said the Chinese had buried the body parts in a common grave in Pudong. We planned every detail of the trip to assure a successful retrieval mission. Our interpreter then phoned the magistrate to thank him and tell him when we would arrive to begin work. I was looking forward to going with my men.

Driving into the excavation area, we were met with the sickening sight and repulsive odor of rotten flesh. The ground around Shanghai is moisture-saturated since it rests at nearly sea level. Even though December cold had somewhat preserved the body fragments, the pungent smell made my eyes water and stomach heave. Many of the Chinese wore face masks as they worked. Not having body-bags in those days, we put the human pieces in eight barracks bags as we tried to reassemble the body of each of the eight airmen. I vividly recall handling a shoe still containing its foot. On the way uptown to the Shanghai mortuary, we drove straight through the city. The vile odor turned every head in the sea of people that lined the streets.

Another letter I received told the story of Lieutenant Billy Seago of West Texas. This P-51 pilot was shot down by the Japanese near Shanghai. The Chinese magistrate reported that the plane had made an emergency but safe landing in some rice patties. However, the young fighter pilot saw the Japanese military headed toward him several hundred yards away across the rice patties and thrust his service knife into his stomach to die rather than face the ruthless Japanese savages. Chinese patriots, much closer to Billy than the Japanese, took his body to a nearby farm and hid it in a hay stack. Not able to find the body, the Japanese towed the plane—riddled with machinegun fire—to the Shanghai Fairgrounds where they displayed it to demonstrate their war power.

I could not bring myself to go with my men on the mission to retrieve Billy's body. Indeed, his story particularly tugged at my heart because I had wanted to be a pursuit pilot, but my mother's wishes kept me grounded. I was gripped with the grim reality that his story could have been mine.

My time in Graves Registration—hearing the stories, reading records, seeing those letters from our faithful Chinese friends, and burying the bodies of my comrades—was by far the most difficult and emotionally taxing segment of my war experience.

With the help of Chinamen, my team and I retrieved what we could find of fallen comrades in their temporary graves in the Pudong area, moving them into body bags and taking them by hand-truck to our army vehicles to be brought back to the American Cemetery in Shanghai.

Remains were placed in numbered caskets—many labeled "Unknown #__."
Each deceased soldier was given a military internment.

In fact, the horror of what I saw, smelled and touched—and perhaps "survivor guilt"—traumatized and numbed me. It shut down my ability to cry or shed tears to this day, some 70 years later.

Chinese Missionaries

The best part of my time in Shanghai began on my first Sunday at an army church service our chaplains had arranged at the Chinese Grand Theater. As I walked out of the theater after the program, a young Chinese man approached me and said, "My name is Mark Zee, and I think you are a Christian." When I assured him I was, he grinned and said he was also. He said, "Would you like to meet my missionary, Miss Broadbridge?" He led me to her apartment a few blocks away. She looked thin and frail, maybe about sixty-five. Nonetheless, she bestowed on me a radiant smile as we greeted each other.

I learned that Miss Broadbridge had been imprisoned in a Japanese concentration camp for three years and had been freed by our army just three days prior to the date the Japanese had chosen to gas her camp. I had great fellowship with Miss Broadbridge and her Chinese Christian friends in the area, both young and old.

During the next seven months, we had frequent prayer meetings and Bible study times at Miss Broadbridge's apartment. I often traveled with Mark Zee and others in my Jeep throughout Shanghai and the nearby towns ministering to various Chinese churches. I soon loved working with those Chinese Christians, and felt strongly that God wanted me to return to China someday as a missionary.

At that same time, Chairman Mao and his communist party were actively introducing communism to China. Even while I was still there, the youth in Shanghai were demonstrating in the streets and marching every day, waving banners supporting the communist way of life.

Shanghai was not known to have malaria-type mosquitos so I stopped taking my Atabrine tablets. Then December 20, 1945, I became very ill and was taken to the 172nd Army General Hospital in Shanghai where I was told I had tertian malaria, the most common type of malaria, one that spikes fevers every other day. I was sent to bed for seven days. The malaria symptoms returned on February 14 of the next year and once again sent me to the hospital. Little by little the fever attacks became less frequent and were finally reduced to about twice a year. Over 70 years later, I still experience occasional bouts but with far less intensity.

I purchased a Chinese costume and had great fun wearing it (shown here with Miss Broadbridge in Shanghai).

Headed Home

In April 1946, three years after I entered the service, I received orders to board a troop ship, but this time they announced my destination: San Francisco...home. I said goodbye to Miss Broadbridge and my many Chinese friends, telling them I hoped to return to minister with them in China. Parting was sad but sweet with the hope of future work in China. But first I had to go back to Penn State to finish my engineering degree and get a Bible education. The Chinese young people begged me to come back as soon as possible. They even printed business cards for me.

My ship left Shanghai and headed east this time. I was happy to find an army chaplain on my ship, as well as a few Christian GIs with whom I had great times of fellowship around God's Word each day.

The Golden Gate Bridge was a beautiful sight heralding our homeland.

I lived in relative luxury in the Foreign YMCA of Shanghai (in comparison with my Ledo tent). Meals were delicious, accompanied by most of the comforts of home.

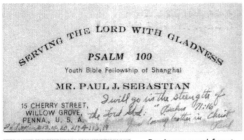

Business card front
(above)

Back of the card:
Chinese characters
for my name and
(on the side)
Psalm 100.

I boarded a train headed east to Fort Dix, New Jersey. Discharged from active duty, I joined most of my comrades in signing an additional three-year contract with the Army Reserve (in case of a recall). My final discharge three years later came just ten days before I would have been assigned to active duty in the conflict with North Korea. Once again, the Lord saw fit to save me from combat experience.

At the time of my arrival back in the States, Dad was employed as a welder at Stucoff Aviation in Trenton, New Jersey. He had helped build hundreds of military gliders that carried our troops by air into combat zones. When he received word that I was being released, he came right over to Fort Dix after work and picked me up. What a great reunion!

Mom couldn't believe I was really home. She made all my favorite foods—roast beef, fluffy mashed potatoes and gravy, cakes and pies and cookies—and we had great times of celebrating my safe arrival home with friends and relatives, praise the Lord!

That summer gave me time to reflect on the past and anticipate my future. I spoke at a few churches, giving testimony to God's goodness. I told stories of

Ecstatic GIs crowded the forward deck of our troopship as we approached our homeland and first sighted the Golden Gate Bridge in San Francisco, California.

His protection throughout my war experience, as well as opportunities to witness for Him, especially my experiences in China and my eagerness to return as a missionary. Speaking at Bethany Baptist Church—our home church—I was dumbfounded and honored when they made me one of their licensed Baptist preachers.

Mom and Dad were not ready for my announcement that I wanted to prepare for missionary work in China. They reasoned with me that I could do much greater good right here in the USA. My Aunt Lillie and Uncle Armon came to visit to plead with me not to go back to China. I felt like Job with his well-meaning friends. Other visitors also came to persuade me to stay at home.

I was grateful to see this army discharge paperwork.

I immediately contacted Penn State about my desire to resume studies and was accepted for the 1946 fall semester. I was convinced my studies at Penn State must be completed—along with Bible school—before I could go back to China. I tried not to be too disturbed by the dissenting advice; after all, friends and family meant well. On the other hand, I tried to not be impatient to finish my studies so I could return to China. I loved the Chinese people and wanted to serve them. Would this dream become a reality…or not?

I posed in full dress uniform for a Chinese portrait artist after the war.

Chapter 5

Penn State and Love

I returned to Penn State in 1946 three years older and much more mature. Although as a freshman I had been a year older than most students, I was now a much older sophomore at 22. Of course, with the war, the ages of students varied greatly. My mind was particularly old, having crossed the world and seen the atrocities of war.

While I had kept to myself as a freshman with a quiet and unassuming personality, I returned to college with honor and accomplishments. I studied hard with a passion to do my best and an urgency to return quickly to the people of China to whom I felt the Lord wanted me to minister.

Soon after the semester began, I noticed a bulletin board flier about a Christian student group on campus. InterVarsity Christian Fellowship (IVCF) held Bible studies every Friday evening and all were invited. I looked forward to the first meeting in Shaub Hall just a few nights later.

After an opening song, new students — about 30-40 — were given the opportunity to introduce ourselves, including hometown and college major. Then an Altoona pastor led the Bible study, and I rejoiced in his exposition of the Word of God. After the meeting, students informally greeted each other and further discussed our ambitions and some told of war experiences. I met Don DeHart who soon became my best friend. Miriam Krebs and Jean Esbenshade introduced themselves; they told me they had visited a Bible conference in Willow Grove (my hometown) that summer and wondered if I ever attended there. Although I admitted I had not, we went on to share an enjoyable conversation. Finding other students with interests and passions common to mine — prayer, Bible study, outreach — filled me with great joy!

In the ensuing weeks, these Bible studies became food for my soul, especially since I could not find a nearby church that taught the Bible as the Word of God. And even though I was generally shy, I felt comfortable with this group of Christian students, even the women.

Our fellowship was always aware that the campus was our mission field, and we tried to attract others to IVCF meetings. Prayer was also very important to us, and several of us met every morning on the top floor of Old Main to pray for fellow students. Don and I were always there. Along with two or three other

My college buddy Don DeHart (right) and I were delighted when our friend Nick Skoberan (middle) found Christ as his Savior at IVCF.

women, Jean was also a regular attender. My interest in her increased, and I began considering my desire for a wife like Jean who knew how to pray with correct theology. I found out years later that she had the same qualification for her future husband.

College Days

Don DeHart, a fellow serviceman also finishing college on the GI bill, lived in a boarding house about a block from mine. Our strong love for the Lord, along with similar values and interests, cemented our friendship. We had a lot of fun together. Often on a Saturday evening as our local grocery store was closing (no sales on Sundays), Don would purchase discounted over-ripe tomatoes, a loaf of bread and a jar of dressing. Then at his house, we enjoyed stacks of juicy tomato sandwiches—a poor man's feast.

We ate most of our meals together. Breakfasts were bought at the New College Diner and consisted of coffee, two pieces of whole wheat toast, butter and jelly for 15 cents, after which we headed off to the IVCF prayer meeting at Old Main.

Don and I often lunched at Fred's Diner on Allen Street. The waiters bellowed abbreviated menu requests from the booths or counter to kitchen, which made for a loud but entertaining environment. For example, "ham, kill

These Chinese Christians were part of my weekly Bible class.

it" meant a well-done burger, "spag" was for spaghetti, and "sos" requested sauce on the side. The patrons were also a source of our amusement. Don nicknamed one of the regulars "Miss Everything" because of her snooty attitude complete with fur coat. He would often whisper in falsetto as she sauntered into the dive, "Here I come, you lucky people." We enjoyed good food and camaraderie at Fred's.

Weekday suppers were spent together at a boarding house downtown where the owner had a passel of children he pressed into service as waiters. He assigned ten students per table. Prior to each meal, ten glasses of milk were carried to the tables by one of his ten-fingered children—no trays needed, just dirty hands and fingernails. If a student dared reach for a leftover piece of

Dr. Henry J. Heydt was founder and first president of today's Lancaster Bible College.

meat, the owner roared, "You had yours," reminding us it belonged to the athlete who was coming any minute from football practice. But meals were tasty and cheap.

Our Penn State student body included quite a few graduate students from other countries, many from China. A few international students attended our Friday night Bible studies. I organized and began teaching a weekly Bible class just for Chinese students, and about 20 or so attended regularly. A few were Christians, and I hope some accepted Christ as their Savior due to our discussions of God's Word.

An IVCF representative visited our chapter each semester to help and encourage us. Bible studies on campus were usually led by a pastor of an evangelical church from nearby Altoona. Occasionally, visiting pastors brought messages. I loved lessons by Dr. Henry J. Heydt, President of Lancaster School of the Bible (LSB), who was an excellent Bible expositor. He answered all our questions using the Scriptures. Each of Dr. Heydt's visits deepened my desire to get my Bible training at LSB.

When Dr. and Mrs. Heydt visited our IVCF group, they were usually driven from Lancaster to State College by Jean Esbenshade's mom and dad. Sometimes the Esbenshades brought along a treat for our whole group, like fresh picked strawberries served with ice cream from the Penn State Creamery. I carefully observed Jean and wished I could date her, but she seemed rather independent and I was afraid she'd say no and tell me she wasn't interested in me.

Each time I heard news reporters comment on communism taking over China, I recalled the

I first met Anna and Martin Esbenshade (Jean's parents) when they brought Dr. and Mrs. Heydt to IVCF.

youth parades I had witnessed in the streets of Shanghai. One such time, I had been crossing the street to get to my office and parade participants had beat on me with their signs and yelled words I could not understand. Just a few months ago, we had freed these people from the Japanese—yet they were now so hostile. I wondered often if I would be able to return to China to serve the Lord.

Outreach at the Penitentiary

About once a month, our IVCF group visited the inmates at Rockview State Penitentiary located between State College and Bellefonte. The facility chaplain, always happy to see us, gave us freedom to lead group singing, present musical numbers (women's trio, men's quartet and an occasional solo), and bring a message from God's Word.

My first visit was scary. Upon entering, our group progressed through several chambers, each of which were unlocked so we could pass through and then locked again behind us. The further I went into the facility, the more uneasiness I experienced. Finally arriving in a large room filled with men of all shapes, sizes, and colors, we were ushered to the platform and introduced.

Soon after I started going on these visits, I was appointed to give the message. My first talk was called "Temporal Things and Eternal Things." I remembered this message from a broadcast by Theodore Epp that meant so much to me.

As an aside, Epp was the founding director and speaker for Back to the Bible radio broadcasts that I listened to daily at Penn State. The previous summer, cousin George—who had taught me many details about radio reception—encouraged me to buy a Hallicrafters Model S-40B Communications Receiver. He showed me how to rig a 100-foot antenna that would allow me to listen to radio programs from all over the world. My favorite station, with the call letters HCJB (Heralding Christ Jesus' Blessings), came from Quito Ecuador. It was on that station I heard the sermons I shared with the men at Rockview.

I spoke for about a half hour. I could never have undertaken a challenge like that in my first year of college, but my wartime teaching experience gave me confidence—I even made appropriate eye contact. The talk was well received by my group. I confessed to Don that I had remembered most of it from listening to Pastor Epp on HCJB radio. Several inmates also came up and thanked me for the message.

Our IVCF group hated to leave Camp Hate-to-Leave-It.

Although I knew I was free to leave at the end of our programs, I still felt great relief at the end of each evening to walk out into the fresh air, a free man. And I would ask God to use the message we had delivered to reach the hearts of the men still in the institution. I was greatly moved by the whole experience.

Special IVCF Events

IVCF sponsored a student outing over Easter break 1947. The Titan Metal Company invited us to use their facilities at Camp Hate-To-Leave-It near their factory in Bellefonte. Their staff prepared the meals and made sure all our needs were met as about 60 students enjoyed a weekend at this lovely retreat center — so aptly named. Gunner Hoagland from IVCF headquarters was the main speaker and told us what was going on at several other campuses in the United States.

Then that July, the father of an IVCF student obtained permission for us to use a state park facility at Parker Dam, just north of State College. Students were encouraged to invite their parents to the event, and — to my great delight — Dad and Mom agreed to come. I was also thrilled that our missionary guest speaker was none other than Miss Mabel Broadbridge, whom I had worked with in China.

Jean Esbenshade had graduated the previous May, and — to my regret — we had said our final goodbyes. But she and her family, including her younger sister Kathy, joined the IVCF group at Parker Dam that July weekend. On Saturday, I borrowed a rowboat, hoping to take Jean for a ride. When I couldn't find her, I invited Miriam Krebs, Jean's best friend, to join me. As she was getting into the boat, Jean and her sister Kathy came along and happily climbed

The Parker Dam IVCF retreat group included: my parents (directly under the cabin window),
Josie (standing on the left, holding her glasses)
with Jeanne beside her and then Miss Broadbridge;
I am hunkered down on the far right with Don DeHart beside me.

In my senior year at Penn State, we enjoyed spending time with Paul and Miriam (Krebs) Apple.

in, too. I thought we all enjoyed ourselves—but for several years afterward, Miriam expressed her displeasure by nicknaming me "Juddy" (which she derived from my middle name, Judson).

Miriam, witty and full of fun, went on to meet and marry Paul Apple. Together they had two wonderful daughters, Amy and Melanie.

Pursuing Jean

Although I always liked being near Jean, I was too timid to do anything about my feelings until it was too late. She had graduated in June. And although I saw her briefly at the Parker Dam IVCF event, I hadn't said anything personal…and a romantic relationship never got off the ground.

Finally, in August, I sat down with my mother and told her about Jean. I shared my concern that I had not pursued a relationship with her and might never see her again.

Mom's eyes twinkled. "Why don't you phone her?"

Now why didn't I think of that!

I placed a long-distance call to Lancaster which at the time involved a live operator. I told the woman I wanted to talk to Jean Esbenshade but did not know her father's first name or her address or phone number.

The operator said, "I have several columns of Esbenshades in the phone book." Then trying to be helpful she asked, "Is he a doctor? Or a preacher?"

I said, "No, he's a farmer."

She said, "Let's try this one." I guess she just started at the top of the second column, because she called J. Martin Esbenshade and hit the jackpot, first try.

Mr. Esbenshade answered, and I began: "I'm Paul Sebastian, a Penn State student from Willow Grove, and I'd like to speak to Jean Esbenshade."

He said, "Jean's not here now. She took her mother shopping."

I could hardly believe this was the right number! So, I asked, "Do you remember me from Penn State?"

He said he did, and we talked about his visits bringing Mr. and Mrs. Heydt to Penn State.

When I asked him about seeing Jean again, he said, "Why don't you come for a visit?"

I could hardly believe my ears. Quickly agreeing and thanking him for the invitation, I admitted I had no car and would need to take the train.

He told me Jean had a car and would meet me at the Lancaster train station in time to get to church for the Sunday morning service.

I later learned that when Jean returned home and heard I had called, she couldn't believe her dad invited me to visit without consulting her. I asked why she had not asked him to call me back and cancel the invitation. She replied with a smile, "Oh, I was interested."

As I got off the train that Sunday morning, this beautiful woman with a lovely smile came toward me—all dressed up and pretty as a picture in her summer dress, heels and wide-brimmed hat. As we walked to the parking lot, Jean apologetically told me the story behind her car. Her dad had given it to her as a graduation gift. Getting the one he wanted was difficult due to a wartime shortage. Few cars were available, so he had chosen a 1947 powder blue convertible Oldsmobile coupe. She seemed embarrassed by it. In my opinion (which I kept to myself), it was obvious that a beautiful woman should drive a beautiful vehicle.

We attended the Esbenshade's church, The Lancaster Gospel Center, and later enjoyed a delicious dinner prepared by her mother at their home on the farm. I returned many times during the next several months, as Jean and I continued to fall in love.

I'm posing here with Jean's 1947 powder blue Oldsmobile convertible and a bouquet of bluebells, one of her favorite flowers.

More About Don

During my junior year, Don drove me to Lancaster to see Jean on the frequent weekends he visited a friend in York. Don and I enjoyed wonderful times of fellowship, especially when we studied the Word of God together.

We both believed in the rapture of the church, but neither of us was sure where it was found in the Bible. We did find it mentioned in 1 Thessalonians 4, but we also thought it must be in Revelation. We would read passages aloud to each other, and so we read through the entire book of Revelation. Zipping through the chapters, we somehow missed noticing the rapture mentioned at the beginning of chapter four. It was years later that I discovered it—and had to chuckle as I remembered our youthful zeal.

I will always be grateful to Don for detecting a fallacy in my spiritual understanding. As a young boy, sometimes my family could not get to Bethany Baptist Church, and my folks would send me to a church around the corner from our house. The Sunday School teacher said, "You need to be good to stay saved." I carried that misbelief with me through high school, the war and college...until Don recognized my error and set me straight using the Scriptures. He showed me that the grace of God which guarantees the security of the believer, is not based on our works but on Jesus' completed work on the cross (Ephesians 2:8-9).

Don and I both studied engineering at Penn State. He wanted to be an engineer, and I wanted to be a missionary. The opposite happened. After graduation, the Lord moved in Don's heart to pursue missions, and God opened doors for me to become the LSB Campus Development Engineer. God's ways are not ours. "A man's heart plans his way, but the Lord directs his steps" (Proverbs 16:9).

So like his father, Don,
Joel (with wife Margaret) DeHart,
has been a major champion and
prayer partner in the writing of this book.

After Penn State, Don studied further at Columbia Bible College, preparing for the mission field. Jean and I knew Garnett LeVan, a home economics graduate from Penn State, and we thought she would make an ideal partner for our friend. Don and Garnett's interest in each other grew as they allowed us the privilege of matchmaking and mentoring. After marrying, they spent their lifetime in Pakistan where they ministered and raised a small tribe of wonderful children. Tim, Joel, Jonathan, Sarah and Phillip are now adults with children of their own, living all over the world and ministering for the sake of the Gospel.

My Parents' Move

In addition to courting Jean in '47 and '48, I put my engineering skills to good use by completing the design for my parents' new home. Before I had left for the war, Mother, Dad and I had spent some time discussing what they wanted in their retirement home. My otherwise boring trip across the ocean to the Pacific theater had been spent thinking through those ideas, formulating plans and getting my drawings checked out by older GIs who were architects in civilian life.

I returned from the war in 1946, and Dad was ready to start his retirement. He wanted to build the house himself! Being a first-class mechanic and

Mom, Dad and Josie loved their new home.

businessman, he had the skills needed. He subcontracted masonry and other tasks to local craftsmen and professionals for the disciplines he lacked. He supervised the entire project and did most of the carpentry. I was tied up at school and only got home every so often.

My whole family rejoiced in God's goodness the day Mom and Dad moved into their new house on the corner of Nash and Everette Avenues in Willow Grove.

Getting Married

I visited Lancaster regularly to see Jean. What a joy! I was intrigued by her family and often heard her parents, Martin and Anna, discussing the possible gift of some of their farmland and buildings to LSB for the development of a new campus. Although I did not participate in their early conversations, I wondered if it would really happen…and hoped it would! Little did I know at the time I was courting Jean that our union would grant me the opportunity to work with the school for more than 60 years in the future.

Love grew steadily. Jean and I wrote to each other every day. One Saturday I drove Jean (in her car) to Sandy Cove camp meeting. The beautiful facility overlooked the Chesapeake Bay in Maryland. The drive was about an hour in each direction, so we had plenty of time to talk. At some point in our conversation, I asked Jean if she would consider marrying me. Her immediate "Yes!" thrilled me (it still does).

Back at State College, the little town with the big school, I headed for Crabtree's Jewelry Shop. I knew nothing about choosing a diamond engagement ring and was thankful for Sam Crabtree who patiently educated me, showing me a selection of beautiful stones. He encouraged me to examine each diamond under his microscope. I settled on the best I could afford; I had scraped together every dollar I could find, savings and all. I remember walking — somewhat fearfully — back to my rooming house with the ring in my pocket, hoping I would not be robbed.

Professor Edward Baldwin, our IVCF faculty advisor, and his wife often entertained the group in their home next to the campus. In December of that year, the Esbenshade family once again brought Dr. Heydt to the campus to teach our group, after which we all enjoyed one of Mrs. Baldwin's delicious meals. Jean and I left the dinner as soon as we dared and headed across campus. Not having a specific plan, I pulled over at the soonest parking possibility. Hands shaking, I presented a small red leather box to Jean. She opened it, looked at the glittering ring, and rewarded me with a beautiful smile. A special kiss followed! Moments later, I looked around to pull back into traffic and noticed I had parked behind one of the cow barns. We still chuckle about that silly detail.

Married by Dr. Heydt on June 5th of 1948, we enjoyed a lovely wedding day in Lancaster. Relatives and friends filled the Gospel Center. My sister, Josephine played the piano and sang. Don DeHart was my best man, and Jean's sister Kathy was her maid of honor. Our reception was held at Hostetter's Banquet Hall in Mount Joy with about a hundred guests who enjoyed a delicious celebratory dinner. We left that day for our honeymoon in Wellsboro, northern Pennsylvania.

During our first year as a married couple, I continued my senior classes at Penn State. We lived in a sweet

Don (middle) was my best man and Nick (right), an usher.

We took a wedding trip to the Pennsylvania Grand Canyon in Wellsboro.

Jeannie looked incredibly beautiful on our wedding day.

little apartment on College Avenue. Jean worked as a bookkeeper at Metzger's Book Store. And we used Jean's powder blue Oldsmobile for transportation.

In the IVCF ministry, four or five Chinese graduate students regularly attended our group meetings, and I continued to conduct their weekly Bible study. With my very limited Bible training, I found it difficult to effectively use the Scriptures to answer their questions. They were very patient with me and faithfully attended the studies, but this experience helped me look forward to further training at LSB.

During my last semester at Penn State, I realized I needed to take one more course over the summer in order to graduate. After the course concluded, I received a letter from the college saying there would be no fall 1949 graduation because only 267 students were eligible, not enough to warrant a formal celebration. I could participate in commencement the following June or receive my diploma by mail. I asked the college to send my diploma immediately, which caused me to feel thereafter as if I never really graduated.

Nonetheless, I could now turn my complete attention to preparing for the mission field...or whatever God had planned for me and my wife. Little did I realize how much of my Penn State education would be put to good use over the next 70 years.

Our tiny kitchen had been created
from a closet.

Jean sits reading in our bedroom
at Penn State.

My official
Penn State graduation portrait.

Chapter 6

Lancaster Bible College

By September of 1949, I was 25 and I had lived through the war, completed my engineering degree, and married a wonderful woman. We moved to Lancaster, where Jean's dad and I worked on sprucing up an apartment in their farmhouse. Jean and I enjoyed living there until we moved to the small house we occupy today.

Life was deceptively peaceful as the world around us experienced devastating events. President Harry Truman announced that the Soviet Union had successfully detonated an atomic bomb on August 29. And on October 1, Chinese Communist leader Mao Tse-tung declared the creation of the People's Republic of China, closing the door to all missionary work—a heartbreaking reality for me.

That September, I enrolled at Lancaster School of the Bible (LSB) which later became Lancaster Bible College (LBC). Classes convened in a building on Mulberry Street in downtown Lancaster from seven to noon, Monday through Friday.

Since classes met only in the mornings, students had the opportunity to work an afternoon job. Unable to locate any openings in the engineering field, I finally settled on becoming a door-to-door salesman as a "Fuller Brush Man." My carrying case of brushes arrived and I was ready to start.

On the very same day, Jean was being interviewed at the local Pennsylvania Unemployment Agency for a bookkeeping job. In filling out paperwork, the interviewer asked her for her husband's occupation. She told him I was a graduate engineer and a student at LSB, looking for a part-time engineering job. He was astonished. That very morning he had received his first-ever request for a part-time engineer.

When Jean came home and told me, I immediately contacted the company, very ready to send back my case of brushes, cleansers, and home care products.

Penn Boiler and Burner was a small business on the Fruitville Pike. I was invited for an interview and introduced directly to the president. He got right to the point, telling me of their problem with a jig built to bend a strip of iron. He explained the process and showed me the malfunction. "Sebastian, if you can solve our problem, the job is yours." I prayed and thought very quickly, as he stood waiting for my answer. When I told him how to modify the jig to make it work correctly, he looked astonished, swore, then said, "You've got the job."

The part-time engineering job at Penn Boiler perfectly fit my schedule and our needs for the next three years.

A Different Kind of Freshman Year

I loved studying God's Word, the basis of every class at LSB. Dr. Henry J. Heydt, founder and first president, taught classes that particularly blessed me

and honed my Biblical world view. I was further thrilled to observe fellow students learning and preparing to go into the world to preach the Gospel. Our total enrollment was 35 students.

President Heydt believed in "living by faith" and that God would supply every need when doing God's work in God's way. His life verse was "I have been crucified with Christ; it is no longer I who live, but Christ lives in me; and the life which I now live in the flesh I live by faith in the Son of God, who loved me and gave Himself for me" (Galatians 2:20).

Founder and president Henry J. Heydt often counseled with students in his office, which doubled as our library.

Therefore, no tuition was charged initially. Students could donate to the school in simple offering boxes located in the entrance lobby. It would not be until the next year, 1950, that the Board of Trustees required each student to pay three dollars per credit for teacher support and operating expenses.

In those early years, President Heydt was the only full-time instructor. Mrs. Heydt was in charge of the bookstore and office, and she taught etiquette. Other faculty members were part-time, usually pastors of nearby churches. They volunteered their time, opened their homes and gave us their hearts.

Many friends of the school were local farmers who donated food for our dormitory students. Other friends of the school and members of the Lancaster Gospel Center supported LSB regularly with their prayers and gifts.

Mrs. Heydt beautifully supported her husband in his role as pastor and teacher, also teaching classes at LSB.

Note the TV8 truck in this photo of the first graduation, outdoors on our new LSB campus, in the late '50s.

Unique Missions Classes and Service

During my second semester, President Heydt called me aside. He explained that one of our missions teachers had just been transferred to a church in the Philadelphia area and could no longer commute to LSB. President Heydt had decided I was qualified to replace this teacher based on my military instructing experience, missions exposure in China, and the fact that I had just taken (the previous semester) the very course he wanted me to teach.

I readily accepted the volunteer appointment and began teaching History of Modern Missions. Because I was older than most students, well-traveled, experienced, and quite comfortable with teaching, this opportunity fit me quite well over the next two and a half years of Bible school…and then some.

Only a few weeks later President Heydt called me aside again. This time he told me of a newly formed missionary agency called the Egypt General Mission (EGM). He wanted me to serve on its council, saying they would meet about four times a year. He added that Charles and Vivian Hoffmeier, who had graduated from LSB the previous year, were two of the missionaries being sent to Egypt by EGM. I knew the Hoffmeiers. Charles had served in Egypt with the US Army during World War II. I saw it as a great opportunity and quickly agreed to serve.

Yet again President Heydt called me aside, this time to ask if I would consent to be the EGM treasurer. I asked what the position entailed, and he said people would send me checks for EGM to support the Hoffmeiers and others. I would deposit the checks and send funds to the missionaries on a monthly basis. I thought that was something I could do, so I said I would be glad to help.

I served the Lord with EGM until 1963 when they merged with Unevangelized Fields Mission (UFM). Becoming a member on the UFM board, I utilized my engineering skills to design an office building at their Bala Cynwyd, PA headquarters. Today the mission agency is known as Crossworld, responsible for over 700 missionaries serving globally. From EGM to UFM to Crossworld, I served a total of 53 years, from 1950 to 2003.

In those days, many deputation presentations included inferior pictures that poorly represented the mission field. President Heydt suggested I teach a course on photography, pointing out the importance for missionaries to

Here is my Structural Design class that met in our Mulberry Street classroom building.

I am teaching a Missionary Building course in the newly renovated attic of the Esbenshade farmhouse.

In the basement of the farmhouse, I taught Principles of Photography and Photo Lab.

illustrate their work with quality images. The course became very popular and was fun to teach. I then added an advanced photo course that laid the foundation for classes I taught to UFM's new missionary candidates years later. This led to a consideration of other practical missions courses we could offer at LSB.

Helping to develop missionaries soon became more important to me than being one, since the door to China was firmly closed; so important that, when my own graduation from

I am discussing the Missionary Offset Printing course with Robert Latham (middle), dean of men and journalism professor, and instructor Orville P. Straton (affectionately called OP).

LSB rolled around in 1952, I gave the milestone very little thought. I was doing the Lord's work now!

Developing a missions curriculum, I enlisted the aid of area "specialists" who agreed to volunteer their time and expertise to train students hoping to go abroad with the good news of the Gospel. We were soon offering a complete array of courses, with a missions faculty of two regular staff members and ten part-time specialists (all volunteers).

By 1953, we offered missions courses such as Bible Basis of Missions, History and Geography of Missions, Comparative Religions, and Customs and Cultures. Robert Latham and I team taught Photojournalism. Courses by other specialists included: Offset Printing & Graphic Arts Lab, Health & First Aid, Missionary Cooking & Homemaking, Auto Mechanics & Engine Lab, Writing and Publishing...and more. I also taught such courses as Mechanical Drawing, Building Design, Water Supply & Sewerage, Surveying, 35mm Photography & Photo Lab, and Science and the Bible.

LSB already offered diplomas in Bible and theology. Then in 1955, a four-year major in Bible & missions was authorized by the Board of Trustees. The program included a mix of three years' worth of our Bible curriculum plus about a year of missions courses.

Even though my initial desire to be a missionary in China had officially fizzled, God had redirected my journey by gifting me with opportunities to equip young missionaries at LSB, assist the EGM mission, and serve with the board of deacons of our local church, the Lancaster Gospel Center. Furthermore, God allowed me to volunteer in these capacities, providing for Jean and me through my part-time work at Penn Boiler and then Richard's Photo Supply (*see the next chapter for more information on my "tentmaking" endeavors in photography*) and through Jean's job at the Simplex

Students gather around the walk-around print processing sink I designed for the Photo Lab course I taught in the farmhouse basement.

During my years in school, I sang in the men's quartet which included (L-R) Dave Heydt, myself, Dave Rutt and Bob Tapper.

Paper Box Company. We considered ourselves blessed.

Expanding the Campus

Each year, student enrollment grew at LSB. We needed more classrooms. We needed more space. In 1952, Martin Esbenshade, my father-in-law, offered the use of his farmhouse. We made a technical classroom in a second-floor attic and converted the entire farmhouse cellar into a photography lab and offset printing labs.

Burgeoning enrollment and tight quarters forced the Trustees to form a search committee to look for buildings in the Mulberry Street neighborhood that could be rented for classroom space. They even investigated a nearby vacated church building. Nothing was available or suitable in downtown Lancaster, so we turned our attention to effective use of the Esbenshade farm, outside of the city proper.

As I talked with my father-in-law about the growing possibility of LSB moving to the farm, I became excited about designing buildings for an official campus.

Malcolm Clinger, a Christian architect in Lewisburg, introduced me to the state officials at the Department of Labor and Industry's Buildings Division in Harrisburg. I was a newly licensed engineer, as Jean had urged me to take the Pennsylvania State Board Examination following my graduation from LSB. I now had a license authorizing me to survey land and design public buildings.

To enhance my architectural and structural engineering knowledge, for several months I commuted one or two nights a week to the offices of Saunter and Castor Structural Engineers in Philadelphia. My mentor was Edwin Castor, an engineer and close friend from my home church in Fox Chase. He taught me how to design foundations, walls and roof structures. I had a wonderful experience learning what I needed to know to design commercial buildings for

The Esbenshade farmhouse is to the far left (among the trees) in this picture of the original farm.

LSB as well as other ministries throughout the years.

In 1953 Dr. Heydt resigned the LSB presidency and moved to New York City to direct a missionary institute for the American Board of Missions to Jews. It was a shock to everyone at the school. Our Trustees organized a search committee. Of the several names presented to the Trustees, Dr. William J. Randolph, who taught Greek and other courses at LSB, was elected as our second president.

One of President Randolph's first responsibilities—along with Dean Wilt—was an initial visit to the annual conference of the Accrediting Association of Bible Schools and Bible Colleges held in Chicago. Our application for membership was submitted, but it took several years of report submissions and campus visitations before LSB finally became an associate member.

In 1954 Martin Esbenshade informed the trustees that he and Anna wanted to give 15 acres of farmland and several buildings to LSB for a campus, in order to provide lots of space for adequate facilities and growth. After expressing the school's appreciation, President Randolph created a campus planning committee of which I became a member.

As often happens with large endeavors, it took several years for plans to come together. The minutes of the Board of Trustees meeting of April 4, 1957 read: *It was moved, seconded and carried that the Board of Trustees accepts the gracious offer by the Esbenshade family of 15 acres of land and existing buildings for a missionary training center for Lancaster School of the Bible.*

Our committee researched the best use of land and purposed a budget to move our operations to the farm. This initial plan included the following. We renovated the farmhouse (fondly dubbed "Old Main") into classrooms on the first floor and offices on the second. We extended Old Main with two classrooms to the north side. And we refurbished a large farm building (previously a tobacco shed) for use as a library on the lower level and a chapel above.

Some of our Corporation members were businessmen in building trades, strategically helpful in the renovation process. We were extremely grateful for those who charged only for materials.

Just before the school took possession of the 15 acres, with farmhouse and outbuildings, Martin and Anna moved into a house located east of the campus on their remaining property. A developer had built this house on speculation a few years earlier, but it had never been occupied. This is another occasion of God's marvelous provision that accompanies His leading in believers' lives. In the ensuing years, the Esbenshades sold more land to the school as the campus expanded.

In 1960, the school was moved from Lancaster City to our new campus. Dormitory students commuted from town until new living quarters could be constructed. We all rejoiced in God's provision of more space.

Changes

Just a year after moving us to the new campus, President Randolph accepted a call to direct the Hebrew Christian Fellowship in Philadelphia. As an

The Trust

J. Martin Esbenshade

Let me digress for a bit to tell you one story of a great man, Martin Esbenshade, an LSB trustee for 28 years, from 1943 to his death in 1971. He was my father-in-law and a very close friend. His trust in God never ceased to amaze me.

During the Great Depression in the early '30s, a prominent bank—The Lancaster Trust Company—closed and kept clients' money, as did most banks during the period following the stock market crash. Martin lost all his savings, which meant he struggled to pay the mortgage on his farm. Martin's uncle held the mortgage and wanted to foreclose in order to pass the farm on to his own son.

Thankfully, Congress passed an act preventing creditors from repossessing land due to bank foreclosures. This act, plus a government grant, enabled Martin to save his farm and continue to pay his mortgage as he was able.

At that time, the Esbenshades were members of a local church that dissuaded members taking any kind of financial aid from the government. The church board told Martin he was required to confess his "sin" before the congregation. Martin was not convinced what he did was sin, and he felt strongly that he could not make a confession in good faith. The church board insisted he confess, so Martin and Anna resigned their membership and looked for another church.

The Esbenshades visited The Lancaster Tabernacle on Duke Street (now known as Grace Baptist Church on Marietta Avenue). They were pleased with Pastor Henry Heydt's exposition of the Word of God and enjoyed fellowship with the congregation. It was here that they first learned of LSB.

I believe one of the greatest benefits of old age is the ability to look back, see the "big picture" and notice the delightful irony that often accompanies God's plans. The building that originally

The Trust Performing Arts Center, 2017
Photo Courtesy of LBC

housed The Lancaster Trust Company—the bank that seized the Esbenshades' money during the Depression—was gifted just a few years ago to Lancaster Bible College by a Christian family. The college has turned the beautiful downtown building—an architectural icon—into The Trust Performing Arts Center, a venue for programs, recitals and speakers—for the glory of God.

The moral of Martin's life: Trust God.

aside, I find it note-worthy that both Dr. Heydt and Dr. Randolph moved from LSB into Jewish evangelism ministries.

At the trustee meeting on July 26, 1961, our academic dean Dr. Stuart E. Lease was called to be our third president. I had graduated from LSB with my friend Stuart, who had gone on for more education in the Boston area and returned later to become our academic dean. Dr. Thomas Figart, a pastor in Baltimore, replaced Stuart as dean.

President Lease led our college through a number of building programs during his presidency. He assigned me, his friend and colleague, the title of Campus Development Engineer, and I was privileged to work on most of those expansion projects.

I had worked at Penn Boiler during my first three years as a student, then Richard's Photo Supply had hired me as a part-time salesman, and finally I had transitioned to my own photo store in Shillington that ran with my part-time supervision. This gave me flexibility to continue teaching morning missions class at LSB and oversee campus building development. Though I was thankful for the photo business that provided for my family's needs, ministry was my passion and LSB was at the heart of it.

The need for campus dormitories was acute, and we finished the first new residence hall in 1963. Our students happily occupied the first new building on campus, named Esbenshade Hall in honor of the Martin Esbenshade family. The cost of this new dormitory (not including furnishings) was $105,000.

In the mid '60s, my father-in-law Martin received notice from the Pennsylvania Department of Transportation that a new Route 222—from Lancaster to the turnpike—would cut through his farm, and his new home would be directly in its path. They told him the highway had been located as far east as possible to minimize loss to the campus. Previously I had designed a new housing development using his remaining farmland; but that project never got off the drawing board due to this new road.

Martin hired a professional house mover to relocate his new home 250 feet to the east—on a new basement foundation. Later, I used that basement for a photo lab. And today the

Kathy (Jean's sister, pictured here with her husband Orie Grove) and Jean gave the Esbenshade home to the college as a living trust.

Alumnus Of Year Honored During LSB Homecoming

Paul J. Sebastian, right, a member of the class of 1952, was honored as the "Alumnus of the Year" during the homecoming activities Saturday at Lancaster School of the Bible. This award, the first such presentation, was made to Sebastian by the Rev. Joseph McCaskey, Denver, left, at a luncheon held on the campus.

Sebastian has been intensely involved in the life of LSB during the past two decades. He served as director of missions and instructor of photo com-

munications, graphic production processes, publications and construction from 1952 through 1963. His interest in the contributions to the school program have continued and he now serves as development engineer, architect, and official photographer for LSB. He also serves as consultant to the public relations department of the school.

Sebastian resides with his wife, the former Jean Esbenshade, and daughter Nancy at 2072 Pine Drive, Lancaster.

In 1968, I received the first
Alumnus of the Year award.

house is the President's Manse, home of Dr. Peter and Paulette Teague.

1966 and 1967 saw two new apartments buildings designed and built. At this time, enrollment exceeded 100 students and increased substantially each year. As we outgrew our chapel and needed a gymnasium, I designed a combination auditorium/gymnasium with a regulation-size basketball court and locker rooms. Folding chairs were set up daily for chapel and stored under the stage.

Personal Challenges

By this time, I had been teaching LSB missions courses for over thirteen years. So, it came as a shock on the first day of classes in September of 1964 when—without any prior notice from the president or dean—my fellow missions teachers and I found that our regular classes were not on the schedule. Brand new courses from a very different approach were being offered by the newly appointed Director of Missions.

I had just been indirectly fired. My ministry was finished. I was stunned.

My mind whirled through memories of the past 13 years. Was my work not good enough? Had I done something wrong? The missions curriculum I designed and the courses we taught had been highly acclaimed by mission executives and appreciated by students who came back year after year to tell me stories of how they had been helped.

The initial shock gave way to feelings of betrayal. Why had no one talked with me about the impending changes?

I went home and took comfort in the Lord and His Word, trying to sort out how "all things work together for good to those who love God, to those who are the called according to His purpose" (Romans 8:28). It took time to accept the changes as God's will, for His glory and my good.

Studying the situation, I learned that over the summer the president had hired a well-known retired missionary and author to head our missions department. His qualifications and experience far surpassed mine. As much as I wished the administration—my friends—had told me about the details as they unfolded, God used this difficult situation to grow in me a new humility, trust and obedience.

All the time I had been teaching at LSB, I had been "tentmaking" in the photography business. Now I could see how God was providing this natural flow into full-time secular work by expanding my photography business. (I tell of my photography career in the next chapter.)

Remarkably, my relationship with LSB continued—a testament to God's sustaining grace—in a different capacity. I continued to serve as the official Campus Development Engineer. And then in 1965, the year after I was replaced in the missions department, I was appointed to serve as a member of the LSB Corporation and accepted gladly. In 1975, I was elected to serve on the Board of Trustees.

The campus grew over the years: 1940's original farm (above), 1980's campus (below). Compare the farmhouse (circles) and shed (squares) in both pictures.

This 2017 aerial photo (2 page spread) of the LBC campus ...

Here is the complete list of campus facilities that bear my fingerprints (to date):

1953	Surveying & campus layout
1956	Old Main (farmhouse)
1957	Chapel/Library (farm shed)
1959	Old Main (addition for classrooms and offices)
1962	Maintenance Building
1964	Esbenshade Hall (as a dormitory and dining hall)
1966	Apartment – south
1967	Apartment – west
1970	Auditorium/Gymnasium
1974	Miller Hall (Student Union)
1988	Apartment – east
1989	Sebastian Academic Center (for classrooms)
2001	Olewine Dining Hall (expansion)
2001	Good Shepherd Chapel
2007	Esbenshade Hall (total renovation)
2008	Good Shepherd Chapel (addition of balcony and acoustics)
2012	Teague Learning Commons
2016	Charles Frey Academic Center (6 academic departments)

Even though challenges arise with each passing year, God has graciously given us many reasons to celebrate His goodness.

In 1973, the Pennsylvania Department of Education approved our new name: Lancaster Bible College (LBC). President Lease maintained that "Bible" should be the center of our name because it is at the center of our education. Praise God it always was and is...pray it always will be.

A Difficult Season

The road was about to get bumpy again.

In 1976 I discovered plans for several new campus buildings that had not been developed or authorized by the Campus Development Engineer...me. I

... was captured by Keith Baum using a photography drone.

began investigating and learned that one of the administrators — along with a trustee who was prominent in the building business — had received President Lease's approval to significantly change our campus without my involvement.

Their plans included two house-type dormitories, a dining hall, an athletic center and a maintenance building. In addition, our auditorium/gymnasium would be converted into a library (with my professional engineering background and as the designer of the building they were changing, I knew the proposed renovation was inadequate for institutional use). I was shocked to learn this entire project would be started soon, at a cost of two and a half million dollars, a fortune in those days. And I knew there was no fundraising plan in place to pay for this project.

When I requested a meeting with President Lease and asked about my findings, he acknowledged what I uncovered was true but declined any further comment. The proposed buildings and accompanying debt went on as planned.

Once again I had been indirectly fired, and I struggled with feelings of frustration and powerlessness. The Spirit of the Lord regularly brought to mind that "a man's heart plans his way, but the Lord directs his steps" (Proverbs 16:9). He reminded me that I was working for Him, not men. Time with the Lord in prayer brought me comfort and strength, as He led me to stay invested in the college.

I was so grateful for Jean during those difficult days. She never flew off the handle in hysteria but listened carefully as I unburdened my heart. Time and time again she shared great common sense and insight, as well as God's wisdom that helped me see the big picture. Together we forged ahead as God revealed each step of the way.

It was difficult to watch the campus change in ways I knew did not reach the level of excellence I had tried to maintain in the past. Yes, we were getting much-needed buildings...but at what cost?

Allow me to jump ahead and say that today most of these structures — complained about for years by students and staff in our Grounds and Building Department — have been razed or renovated and other quality facilities added to our campus. In fact, in 2016, LBC was ranked by Christian Universities

Online as one of the 50 most beautiful Bible college campuses.

While that building project was going on in the '70s, the faculty asked for a meeting with the Executive Committee of the Board of Trustees, of which I was secretary. We were told how poorly the president was managing the college. Prolonged illness and family struggles had been sapping his strength and diminishing his vision for the college for quite some time.

The committee confronted the president with the complaints. Then I met with my friend privately and suggested he resign…but he did not. Sadly, only a short time later he was removed from office. It was difficult for the whole college family.

Rebuilding and Prosperity

Thus began the search for a new president. Several fine men of God were considered. Some of us knew Dr. Gilbert A. Peterson when he was academic dean at Philadelphia College of Bible. We learned he had moved on to Evangelical Free Divinity School in Deerfield, Illinois. Two of our trustees traveled to Deerfield and asked him to come to Lancaster to meet with our Board and faculty and look at our situation.

The board of trustees asked Dr. Peterson many questions when he arrived. I remember the first question asked by chairman Ralph Good: "How long have you had that beard?" It was a question related to the times and local culture; our students were expected to be clean-shaven.

Without a second's hesitation, he replied, "Since puberty." We later came to appreciate his direct answers…and to accept his beard.

I distinctly remember raising the question, "Why do you want to be our president?"

Dr. Peterson immediately replied, "I don't want to be your president; I just came to help you."

He stayed a few days visiting every department and talking with board members, faculty, staff, students and friends of the college. His comments and recommendations greatly encouraged us. We diligently prayed together that the Lord would send us the best man to lead us out of our troubles and help us move forward to be the kind of college that would fully glorify God.

Within a few days following Dr. Peterson's return to Deerfield, he got back in touch with us. The Lord had led him to accept our offer of the presidency. We were elated.

In 1979 Dr. Peterson became the fourth president of LBC. Little did we know, with God's help he would accomplish just what was needed in every area of our college. President Peterson faced

Dr. Peterson and I hold a Sebastian Miniature® Conestoga Wagon, an LBC exclusive.
Photo courtesy of LBC

what seemed to be an insurmountable task: our indebtedness (two and a half million dollars with no plan for repayment), low faculty morale and low status with the accrediting associations and the Pennsylvania Department of Education...

By 1994, 15 years later, President Peterson had completely transformed the college. Due to plenty of hard work and excellent leadership, LBC was completely debt free, with full accreditation and full approval from the Pennsylvania Department of Education. He enlarged the Board of Trustees and Corporation and added many new very qualified faculty and staff members.

From the beginning of his tenure, President Peterson said LBC was Lancaster County's best kept secret. With perseverance and determination, he put the college on the map, known and respected locally and around the world.

Dr. Peterson was our first president who was fully qualified for the office. He not only had the executive leadership experience and skills; he also possessed an earned doctorate in education.

Under his direction, in 1988, we erected our third campus apartment building. Then in 1989, we built and dedicated the Sebastian Academic Center—a much needed classroom building. President Peterson always wanted LBC to have a proper Chapel and was very diligent in perfecting every detail of the building, naming it the "Good Shepherd Chapel." It was dedicated in 2001.

Dr. Peterson served as our president from 1979 to 1999, and then continued as the first chancellor of Lancaster Bible College until 2005. I feel one of his greatest contributions to the college was to recommend our academic dean, Dr. Peter W. Teague, (who had the complete support of our faculty) to be named our next president. No other candidate was even considered, and Dr. Teague was elected the fifth president of Lancaster Bible College.

The Legacy Continues

Like his predecessor, President Teague possessed extensive experience and education. Prior to involvement at LBC, he served at the Christian School of York as Director of Development for four years and Superintendent for 19. With a Doctorate in Education, he taught in eight colleges, authored several books and was involved in leadership positions in many organizations and associations of higher education. He was also a respected professor and the Dean of Education at LBC before becoming our president.

Throughout the past 17 years President Teague has loved the Lord and LBC. He has prayerfully used his education, knowledge and wisdom to lead our 300 dedicated and qualified faculty and staff. He has added numerous undergraduate majors, as well as graduate

Dr. Teague stands with Nancy who spoke on my behalf (I was ill) during the rededication of Esbenshade Hall.

The Chapel Window

Coming onto the LBC campus, one of the first things a visitor notices is the Good Shepherd Chapel with its Early American architecture and prominent rose window. Three noticeable design features I contributed to the chapel include the unique proscenium (front of the stage), the bust of founder and first president Dr. Henry J. Heydt, and the rose window.

It was only as I wrote this book that I made the connection between this rose window and the one my father helped create in the National Cathedral. As a blacksmith, he had been commissioned to create the iron framework to hold the stained glass created by artist Lawrence Saint. As a second-grader, I traveled with my mother to Washington D.C. to watch my father install the window. Years later, I would complete a similar project.

Dad's framework holds the stained glass for "The Last Judgement" at the Washington National Cathedral.

My framework, over the LBC chapel window, depicts the radiant glory of the cross of Christ.

David Lynch, architect for the Good Shepherd Chapel, designed a large round window in the south wall of the LBC chapel. The original hope for a stained glass window was cast aside as we peeled back the budget. Well, maybe we could find a donor who would be excited about funding the stained glass to make it a showpiece. Unfortunately as the building construction progressed and plans changed here and there, we realized that the window would not be seen from the inside. This made high-priced stained glass an even more unnecessary expense.

Looking at the massive plain window from the front of the campus, I wanted to do something to make it seem more aesthetically pleasing. It was then I formulated the idea to put a mask on the window.

I patterned my design according to a study of many stained glass rose windows and took it to a supplier who made the mask out of white aluminum. Transported to the college and installed in pieces, the mask was applied to the outside of the window with special aircraft two-sided adhesive tape.

The window mask is white against the dark window by day and back lit so you see light through the glass at night. The effect is stunning.

And what a delight to know that both Dad and I were involved with a rose window project in our lifetimes!

degrees and certification programs, including PhD degrees. LBC now ministers at six locations: Lancaster, PA; Philadelphia, PA; Memphis, TN; Boca Raton, FL; Capital Seminary in Greenbelt, MD and Uganda, East Africa.

This unprecedented growth required additional facilities at our Lancaster campus. President Teague continually encourages my involvement and utilizes my expertise. Under his direction, Olewine Dining Commons was enlarged, the Good Shepherd Chapel was completed and later renovated, and Esbenshade Hall was completely renovated to provide executive offices, a student enroll-ment department, student finance offices and a state-of-the-art internet technology center.

And a high-tech learning center that contains our library of over 382 thousand books and items was built and named the Teague Learning Commons, nicknamed the TLC. Our most recent building is the Charles Frey Academic Center.

Sadly, Old Main — the Esbenshade farmhouse, used more than 50 years for classes and offices — had to be razed due to non-compliance with current building codes. All these changes were made with God's help, successful fundraising programs, and the prayer and gifts of faithful friends of the college.

Playing with Clay

After President Teague transitioned to headship of the college, I began thinking of a way to honor our founder and first president. I suggested to President Teague that we make a bronze bust of Dr. Heydt, whom I had known very well and had photographed often. Although I had not done much sculpting, I felt sure I could produce what was needed. He agreed and asked me to start at once. My wife Jean knew Dr. Heydt even longer than I did and offered her help. Sculpting the clay head progressed well. After three months of part-time work on it, I was ready for others who knew him to tell me if it was a good likeness.

Betty and Lilton Clark, early graduates of LSB, came to look and were happy with it. Dr. Lease was in town visiting friends and he stopped in. He said, "That's good. It's nice to see him again." But the real test came when Henry's son David came from Florida to check on the progress. He seemed very

The Heydt sculpture greets visitors and friends in the Chapel.

pleased with the bust, saying it looked so very much like his Dad.

I worked with a foundry studio in Ephrata that made an excellent bronze casting from my clay model. We mounted it on a pedestal of black granite and placed it in the lobby of the Good Shepherd Chapel. We intentionally positioned it between the door to the Prayer Chapel and the door to the Board of Trustees room so that all who pass through these doors will remember our humble beginnings, our foundation in God's Word and our godly heritage.

Presently, President Teague continues LBC's tradition of excellence and integrity, along with his qualified trustees, administrators, cabinet, faculty and staff. For almost 20 years, he has led our college to great accomplishments: increased enrollment in undergraduate programs; multiple masters and doctoral degrees; locations in four states, with many courses offered online; operation of our Capital Seminary and Graduate School in the greater Washington Region; our Pastors Discipleship Network in Uganda, East Africa; and our Trust Performing Arts Center in downtown Lancaster.

It is my current privilege to now honor President Teague with a bust of himself that was completed shortly before this book's release.

The clay original was cast in

Nancy and I pose with the clay bust of Dr. Teague; note the enlarged photo of him on the wall behind us, as well as Dad's ironwork.

bronze at Art Research Enterprises in Lancaster. The mounted bust will eventually be placed in the Teague Learning Commons (TLC) as a reminder of God's grace and faithfulness to the college through President Peter Teague.

It thrills me to write about LBC's amazing history and the college's present position of blessing and greatness. The college has grown from 35 students in my freshman year to more than 2000 students today. And our alumni are fulfilling God's purposes for their lives, living by a Biblical worldview, and proclaiming Christ by serving Him all over the world. For all of this I give God the glory! How thankful I am to have been a part of the college's growth for more than 60 years, having encouraged more than 4,000 alumni.

The completed bronze cast of Dr. Peter Teague will reside in the TLC.

Chapter 7

A Photography Career

While my greatest life passion has been God's work—especially in missions and through LBC—I have also loved photography. I learned a unique focus on the world around me the day my cousin George introduced me to the camera. Ever since that summer of 1937—80 years prior to the release of this book—I have seen my world in terms of a picture. Even without a camera in my hands, I capture images in my mind's eye.

That summer's amazement turned into a lifelong love of photography. George continued mentoring me throughout my school days. In high school, I earned money taking sports pictures. I brought home many remarkable images from the war. And since then I have captured family and business events, vacation scenes, and countless pictures of people. A lifetime of memories were reawakened as I filtered through box after box of slides, negatives and prints to choose just a few select images for this book—what a challenge and delight!

From George's initial lesson that summer, God has grown my photo hobby into "tentmaking," work that provides financial support for a ministry-based life. By God's sovereign grace, the photo industry has afforded me the honor of serving the Lord throughout the years.

My Job Path after Graduation

A few days before my graduation from LSB in 1952, the president of the boiler company where I had worked for the previous three years called me into his office. "Sebastian, I know you are almost done with school, and I want you to work here full-time. I want your mind 24 hours a day."

My immediate silent prayer went something like: "Lord, save me from this man!" He was one of the most ungodly persons I have ever encountered. When I shared my testimony with him months before this incident, he had smugly replied that God answers his prayers and gives him everything he wants—end of conversation. Most regrettably, I seemed to get nowhere in trying to talk to him about the Lord.

I cordially thanked him for his offer and requested a few days to think about it.

Starting as a salesman at Richard's Photo Shop, owner Red gave me a panel body truck as my first company car, very handy for delivering goods and carrying demonstration materials (unknown artist lettering the vehicle).

He agreed.

The very next day I stopped for film at Richard's Photo Shop, a store in Lancaster I frequented. Owner "Red" Richard's face lit up when he saw me, and he motioned me into the back room. "Paul, come here for a moment. I've got something wonderful to share with you."

He explained that the Eastman Kodak Company had offered him some additional dealerships to sell industrial photographic products in the area...if he had the right sales staff. He wanted me for his team, assured me he thought I could handle the job, and told me I could start immediately. Sometimes the Lord answers a prayer very quickly; this was one of those times!

However, teaching at LSB was my mission and passion. I had been praying that God would continue to allow my "tentmaking" to provide for my family as I poured my life, knowledge and experiences into students heading to the mission field. I told Red about my weekday teaching commitment from seven to ten o'clock in the morning, Monday through Friday.

Red assured me that scheduling would not be a problem. "Paul, I know you can do the job."

I sincerely thanked him and went home to pray with Jean about this job possibility. As we prayed and thought together, God made it clear to us that I should work at Richard's. I accepted the position (and most gratefully resigned from the boiler company).

Some Ups and Downs from My Time at Richard's

That November I began the new job with a five-day training course at the Kodak company in Rochester, NY. I returned home and immediately started calling on portrait studios, graphic arts shops and industrial companies in Lancaster, York, Harrisburg, Lebanon and Reading while continuing to teach part-time at LSB.

I remember that 1952 was the year Queen Elizabeth also began a new job...governing the United Kingdom. Seems we are both still working in our respective fields.

Sales went well for me. I was very interested in meeting customers and learning the way they used photography in their business. Finding ways to help them with their technical problems intrigued me, and I had opportunities to help them design their own lab facilities. After repeated visits, I was often able to design special equipment to help increase their efficiency and lab safety.

In time, we began selling a variety of product lines. Company representatives from these companies would visit our store and often make customer calls with me. This helped me learn about new products and incentives, while keeping up-to-date on our current inventory. I also regularly attended dealer training sessions and conventions.

One day in 1953 Bob Castleman, a sales representative from the Polaroid company, stopped in to show me their latest Model 95 camera that produced a picture in just 60 seconds. "Paul, this will revolutionize photography." He demonstrated, and sure enough, out came a black and white photo within 60 seconds. It was a large heavy camera, about three times bigger than my Dad's favorite camera. And each print required a protective layer of lacquer applied as the final step—very messy.

"Bob, that will never sell."

He responded with zeal, "It's the wave of the future! Paul, you ought to buy a block of 100 shares of stock at only seven dollars a share. You'll never miss it and you'll be rich in no time."

I thanked him but added, "Bob, that will never sell. Everybody today is looking for a small camera to hang around their neck."

These were two bad decisions on my part. That Polaroid camera I snubbed took the world by storm. And regrettably I chose not to invest in Polaroid stock at the time Bob suggested it. Soon after our talk, he became a very rich vice president for Polaroid. Had I prayed for the Lord's wisdom as I considered his suggestions, perhaps I would be wealthy as well...then again, that might not have been God's plan for me.

This next story further illustrates my reluctance to embrace current trends. I had just stepped out of Richard's on a very hot and humid day when one of my friends drove up in his new Chevy station wagon. He called me over to take a look at his prize. Engine still running, he pointed out various new features. Then he showed me some odd vents. "Paul, put your hand here." An adjustable nozzle emitted very cold air and froze my hand. "This is air conditioning!"

I shivered. "That's cold! I wouldn't want it blowing on me." How wrong can a fellow be? Today I cannot function in the heat of summer without air-conditioning! I'm sure you will agree.

Despite these somewhat sad choices due to my cautious nature, there was a time when my clean lifestyle was—in a very small way—rewarded. A sales training event in Philadelphia attracted photo salesmen from several states. The discussion following each presentation included an unprecedented amount of swearing. Someone suggested we set up a "kitty" to limit the swearing. Each infraction cost a fine of ten cents. It worked; discussions became much more profitable. At the end of the day, all our names were placed in a hat to win the kitty, and—you guessed it—they picked me! The following Sunday, I enjoyed putting their guilt money (all $4.70 of it) into the church offering plate.

Connecting with Oscar H. Hirt

In early 1955, Eastman Kodak Company held a training event at a very swanky hotel in New York City. After the morning sessions, we were treated to a delicious luncheon in a huge ballroom where long tables were set in splendid array. I picked a place and sat down, unfamiliar with anyone except two of the Kodak representatives I had met previously.

I noticed out of the corner of my eye that the fellow to my left had lowered his head and was sitting motionless. I thought to myself, "He's either ill or praying." As he lifted his head, we made eye contact. As we exchanged greetings, we delighted in learning we were brothers in Christ.

The man, Oscar H. Hirt, Jr., explained that he worked with his father (Sr.) who had started O.H. Hirt Photo Supplies in downtown Philadelphia in 1912. We exchanged business cards and enjoyed further fellowship during the meal. Oscar was very interested in my work and background, and especially my involvement and teaching of missions classes at LSB. As we parted to go to different afternoon sessions, we expressed pleasure at meeting and hope to see each other again.

Some months later, Oscar phoned me and wanted to know if I thought central Pennsylvania had enough potential business to support another photo dealership without hurting Red Richard's business. I thought about the possibility of partnering with Oscar, but had to admit to him that I did not believe there was sufficient territory available. He understood and expressed regret that we could not work together.

Not long after the conversation with Oscar, my boss called me into his office. I had been a salesman at Richard's for over three years. Red glanced at me and then down at his desk. "Paul, my accountant says I'm $80,000 in debt." (I later thought, knowing a little about his lifestyle, that he must have overspent on vacations, cars and boats.) "I have to cut my overhead immediately in order to stay in business." As he continued to stare at his desk, he said, "I'm sorry, Paul." Then I realized I was some of that overhead he had to cut. He explained how much he appreciated my work and told me to take all the time I needed to get a new job.

I thought to myself: Lord, please help me again. And He did!

That very same night, Kodak representative Ed Feathers called me at home—as he often did—to set up sales calls for the next day. I recounted what Red had just told me about his financial trouble…and concluded that I would be looking for a new job.

Shocked, Ed immediately said, "We can't lose you, Paul. Kodak has a lot invested in you." Then he added, "You know Oscar Hirt. I want you to contact Oscar tomorrow, before you take any other job. Please phone him in the morning." When I told Ed that I didn't want to work in Philadelphia where Oscar was, he suggested Reading as a potential Kodak territory.

The next day, after phoning Oscar, I went to Philadelphia to see him. He listened intently and then said, "Let me see what Dad thinks." After a few minutes in his father's office, he returned and stretched out his hand. "We're in business!" Over the next few hours, he laid out a plan of how he and his dad would finance a branch operation for me in the Reading area.

Just a couple of days later, Oscar met me in Shillington, a suburb on the Lancaster side of Reading. With the help of a real estate agent, we found a suitable place to locate our new business. The next day he filled my station wagon with photo supplies from his Philadelphia store, and I returned to Shillington to stock my warehouse and begin making sales calls on businesses and industries. I was careful not to contact any of Richard's accounts as I searched for sales.

Jean and I named the company O.H. Hirt Graphic Reproductions, Inc. We were delighted to be immediately successful—and, I still had enough time to continue teaching part-time at LSB! Jean resigned her job at the Simplex Paper Box Company and became our business manager. My father-in-law, Martin Esbenshade—retired from farming—came on board to manage our warehouse and make deliveries.

31 North Miller Street housed our first Oscar H. Hirt photo shop in Shillington. This was my sales force, standing with Oscar (right).

Yet again I found myself praising God for His direction and provision.

Continuing a Passion for Missions

I developed a close friendship—as well as a business relationship—with Oscar Hirt Jr., and soon learned of his involvement with The Bible Club Movement (BCM now stands for Bible Centered Ministries International with headquarters in Lancaster). President Bessie Trabor had just announced her retirement. Oscar, serving at the time as treasurer, was elected to the presidency. He appointed me to the board in 1966, and I was later named secretary-treasurer. I served with BCM from 1966 to 2005, a total of 39 years.

The Lord also allowed me to serve for a few years with Hal Street, Director of Evangelical Literature Overseas, a mission dedicated to helping Christian organizations produce effective Christian literature around the world. He took special interest in our LSB offset printing courses and spoke in our chapel several times. Hal also admired my photography and gave me many assignments over the years.

Not only have my photo skills come in handy for various mission needs, but over the years I've been able to design numerous buildings and lent my engineering expertise to many missionary agencies and churches. I have been so grateful for continued opportunities to serve the Lord through various mission and ministry opportunities, even though He did not assign me to overseas work in China.

I am shown here with Mr. Hirt Sr (90 years old) and Oscar Hirt (Jr), my lifelong friend and ministry partner at BCM.

Dad Esbenshade is in our Shillington warehouse reviewing orders to be filled.

Designs and Inventions

In those early days, I provided customers with solutions to their problems and the best products for their needs...even if that meant inventing something new.

One of my early inventions helped small photo shops afford a new Kodak and du Pont film product for use in drawing reproduction and printed circuit industries. The film was of exceptional quality but could only be processed in one of their expensive automatic machines. I invented a manually operated tabletop processor. My contacts at Kodak and du Pont were impressed and highly encouraging. They told me I had something that should significantly enable small shops to use their film.

Within a year of the original design, I acquired both US and Canadian patents for my manual "Wash-Off Film Processor" to protect my invention. But by the time I exhibited my processor at shows and conventions and sold a dozen, the market changed once again as a newer and better process came along.

As I continued to invent products in the ensuing years, I decided not to request any additional patents, as I could not have afforded court costs and legal expenses to defend my designs if faced with fraudulent competitor copies. This challenged me to create one-of-a-kind designs that would be difficult to replicate.

In 1957 Oscar phoned to tell me of a new material, excellent for resisting acids, that could be used for photo darkroom equipment. He told me to look at

Our Shillington office was small but efficient; in the foreground is a short-term associate, and at the back desk is longtime clerk and friend, Marcella Landreth.

Friday evenings, when Roy Landreth (Marcella's husband) came home from a week of traveling sales, we would all go out to the Holiday House in Reading for a scrumptous dinner. At the table you see (L to R) Roy, myself, Marcella, Nancy and Jean.

the new tanks on display in his Philadelphia showroom. "It's called PVC." Polyvinyl chloride plastic cannot be damaged by photo chemicals.

Delighted with this material that worked so well in the darkroom, I took new ideas for hand-fabricated equipment to Bill Mihm, a gifted craftsman in

Since LSB could not afford the process camera needed for the printing course I began teaching in 1954, I designed and built one. I found a lens that could project a same-size 16"x20" image and rolled along a 14' track between copy board and moveable film board. A lens cap was the shutter, with exposure times of ten or twelve seconds. This invention worked perfectly for the eleven years I taught the course. In this photo, OP Straton stands by our camera in the 1952 renovated cellar of the Esbenshade farmhouse.

Much later my dad built this copy camera I designed for the UFM field office.

southern Jersey. He agreed to make any item I could design. I realized this was the niche market I had been looking for, where my competition would find it difficult to duplicate my inventions. And this time I was right!

For almost 60 years now, I have designed and manufactured film processing sinks, walk-around print processing sinks with print washers, and ventilation systems. These Sebastian Darkroom Products are found in many art schools and universities across the country, and I am privileged to design and consult in the industry to this day.

God prepared me for this work through the bunks I designed and built with my neighborhood buddies, through the photo lab I set up as a 13-year-old in my basement, and through the classes I taught at LSB. I find it so amazing to piece together God's plan and see His incredible faithfulness. And I continue to be thrilled at how my inventions fit the needs of those who use them. Thanks be to God!

The Lab

RCA, a large electronics company in Lancaster, was one of my best customers. One day as I delivered photo supplies, they asked if I could take industrial photos at their plant and provide overnight processing delivered the next morning. I said yes and immediately set up a basement darkroom in the new Pine Drive home Jean and I had recently purchased. Then RCA engineers began giving me additional film they exposed, requesting overnight print service. The quantity of work was so great I had to employ a friend, Bill Hollinger, to help keep up with this demand.

Dad & Mother Esbenshade moved their house in the early '60s due to the highway development program (mentioned in the last chapter) and graciously offered us the use of their new basement. We moved our lab there and named the enterprise Commercial Photographic Service (CPS). I enjoyed the privilege of designing a much larger facility than I had been using at home. We were able to not only produce more work but also offer additional services. With this new facility, we operated day and evenings with sometimes as many as six technicians. Having a commercial studio allowed us to provide fine portraits at no charge to those in Christian ministries. I cannot count the number of missionary prayer card photos produced in the studio and processed in the lab.

A natural extension of being a photographer is being asked by family and friends to take wedding pictures. The number of weddings I shot is also something I find hard to recall. Many of these were processed at the lab.

I am profoundly grateful for the many staff members who efficiently and effectively ran CPS for more than 30 years. The lab was finally sold to Bob Wiker and moved to Route 30, the Lincoln Highway, in 1998.

Relocating Our Business

Jean and I continued to live in Lancaster and travel to our business in Reading for many years. Our daily commute, on the old Route 222 (renamed Route 272 when a super highway was created later), was a 35-minute ride in good traffic. Each morning Jean would accompany her Dad to the office, and I would follow later after teaching my classes and meeting with contractors concerning any buildings under construction on the LSB campus. Martin would make his deliveries. And I would drive Jean home at the end of the workday.

In 1961, after 13 wonderful years of married life, the Lord gave us a daughter. Little Nancy came along with Jean, who reduced her hours at the Hirt company. After Nancy began school, she was cared for by Jean's mother or Margaret Uhler, our regular babysitter, a dear friend and the nurse at LBC. Jean generally worked on Mondays and Fridays.

One terrible morning in 1971, Dad Esbenshade came into the office and sat down after unloading a big shipment of Kodak goods in the warehouse. I seldom saw him sit down at work. Surprise turned to alarm when I noticed him rubbing his chest.

I asked him if I could take him to a doctor to check him over.

He quietly said that he'd be okay, that he just needed to sit down awhile.

When he didn't seem to improve over the next few minutes, I offered to take him to the hospital.

He declined but asked me to drive him home. We left immediately.

Reaching his home, I called his doctor while his wife helped him into bed. Then I excused myself because I was already late for a committee meeting at LSB.

Soon after the meeting began, someone tapped me on the shoulder and whispered, "You better go to the Esbenshades. Martin is dead."

I was shocked! I rushed to comfort my mother-in-law and phoned Jean who was still back in the Shillington office.

When I called Oscar to tell him Dad Esbenshade had passed away, he grieved with me over our great loss. At the same time, we rejoiced that Dad was with the Lord.

Later in the same conversation, I relayed news I had just learned about Red Richard going out of business. This meant that a local Kodak dealership was available. As we discussed the ramifications of these recent events, Oscar and I agreed this would be an ideal time to move our Shillington operation to Lancaster.

Jean and I sadly said good-bye to our local Shillington employees and relocated the business to Lancaster, directly across Eden Road from Lancaster Bible College. I rejoiced that God provided a location so convenient for commuting between my two workplaces.

In early 1980, Oscar decided to

Bill Hollinger, who began as my in-home basement lab technician, worked for me as an outside representative and took over Dad's work in the warehouse when we moved to Lancaster.

Jean is working at her desk in the new Lancaster location; behind her are a few of the photographic memorabilia that led to my massive collection.

retire from business and told me he wanted to sell the Lancaster branch to us. Oscar's Dad had recently passed away at 100, and the business in Philadelphia had been sold to Williams, Brown and Earle. Oscar himself wanted to shift his attentions from business to full-time ministry.

Jean and I understood and were able to make arrangements to take over the business. Because of the increasingly technical nature of photography, we decided to rename the business HIRTECH. The new name was well accepted, and I liked the fact that it preserved the name Hirt, honorable in our industry since 1912.

Over the next 20 years, various employees, managers and professionals joined our team, moved on, and the staff turned over again and again. I loved photography, products and designing, and we shared meaningful relationships with most of our staff and our clients; but people problems wore me out. Jean and I began feeling it was time to look for a buyer for the business. We had added a showroom and rental section, as well as other features, and it was time for a younger person with new ideas to take HIRTECH into the future.

We were grateful to sell the business to long-time friend, Dennis Fahnestock. We grieved with him when the digital age and changing photographic industry forced him to close several years later.

Interesting Twists in Photo Lab Design Work

In the late 1990s, Bill Mihm developed a fatal illness. Unfortunately, when his son took over the business, the new fabrications of my photo darkroom product line did not match the quality of Bill's earlier work. I had to find and train another PVC fabricator.

After quite a search, I met Ken White of Exodus Plastics near Reading. Ken now creates my products with great precision and will travel thousands of miles to complete installations. Added

Joanne and Jim Dissinger were faithful HIRTECH associates and friends for many years. She satisfied customers and suppliers as our Customer Relations and Purchasing Agent. He left a good job at RCA to join our little company as a top-notch salesman; we shared many adventures on the road and at conferences.

bonuses to this arrangement include Ken's strong testimony as a Christian businessman and the fact that he has become a very good friend.

I created mechanical drawings for almost 60 years using pen and ink on paper on a large drawing board. Now architects were saying, "Paul, we've passed into the computer age. We need computer-generated drawings." I was 72 and faced an uphill climb. To say this was a difficult transition is a gross understatement.

Kent Bookman, an AutoCAD professor at York Technical Institute, became my tutor, coming to my home two nights a week for six months to teach me computer technique, most specifically the engineering software called Computer Aided Drafting (CAD). I am pleased to say I made the grade and kept my architects happy.

Dennis Fahnestock and I shake hands in front of the HIRTECH Showroom.

Today I prefer CAD to drawing on paper. Customers regularly have changes, and they often change the changes. Correcting drawings, making duplicates and storing designs for future use is easier, quicker and space-saving with a computer. Plus, I can send a drawing to a client by email with the click of my mouse.

I still ask Kent to come over and help me with upgrades and challenges from time to time. How grateful I am that God made our minds to continue learning over the entirety of a lifetime!

When Jean and I sold HIRTECH, we kept our line of Sebastian Darkroom Products. Our best dealer was California Stainless Manufacturing in Camarillo, CA. They had made premium darkroom sinks of stainless steel for many years. President Jim Carr was a great communicator and he always paid my invoices even before the due dates.

Ten years ago, I decided it was time to cut my workload and semi-retire. The natural choice of a buyer for our product line seemed to be California Stainless. Jim and his brother Randy immediately accepted my offer and agreed that I could continue to design lab plans and create new products for him. Today Jim is one of my best friends as well as a very generous employer.

Jean and I continue to praise God for our fabulous relationships with

Karen and Jim Carr have become very dear friends in addition to stellar business associates, along with Jim's brother Randy of California Stainless.

business associate and friends—and for His goodness and guidance over the years.

Business Lessons

My business office has also been my classroom many times. I learned some things the hard way…by experience.

One spring, I hired a young man fresh out of high school and anxious to start working. I thought I could make a salesman of him because he had a great personality. I trained him to sell Kodak's Verifax office copiers. It wasn't a complicated product, and he caught on right away. I made a few sales calls with

A formal portrait with
the three tools of my trade:
camera, sliderule, and Bible.

him at nearby businesses. I showed him how to fill out our weekly sales report which he was to turn in when he picked up his pay (we paid in cash in those days). He assured me he was ready to start out on his own. I was impressed.

Week after week he turned in very complete detailed report of all the calls he made. I noticed his customers always said they would place an order in the fall, but his reports were the best I had ever received from any of my salesmen. I was so busy in the office, I failed to make calls with him and go back to close any of his great contacts.

A few months later, the young man sent me his resignation, explaining that he was going to college in September. I gave his leads to my other salesmen to follow up. All of them reported that not one of his "customers" had any record of his visits! And so, I learned to be more attentive to my sales team.

Over the years Jean and I had many fine and trustworthy employees: Art Hunsberger, Marcella Landreth, Fern Mauer, Jim and Joanne Dissinger, and of course Martin Esbenshade—to name a few. But we also had trying times with unfaithful staff.

While in Shillington, our company was robbed. Without breaking any locks, the thieves came into the shop after hours and took about a dozen high-priced German cameras and many other things. We learned later that the culprits, upon hearing of the police investigation, became afraid, drove to the middle of the Columbia-Wrightsville Bridge and threw the stolen goods into the Susquehanna River. What a waste! When the police determined that one of our employees had used her key to let her friends into the office, the culprits all went to jail but restitution was never paid to us. Unfortunately, business losses of this nature are far more common than one might think.

Later in Lancaster, we had two other misadventures (that come to mind).

One evening my night lab manager phoned to say he had discovered something I should know about. I drove over to the lab immediately where he showed me a stack of film holders and finished work belonging to a particular customer – with no trace of paperwork for the job. He told me he had seen this many other times, unbilled work for this customer. His story convinced me that my day manager was fudging the books, and he asked me what I was going to do about it. I told him I would have to fire the person responsible.

There were fun times as well as hard lessons. This caricature of me was sketched at a photographic convention.

I returned home very disturbed and could not sleep that night. The next day I went to the lab before the day manager's normal arrival. When he showed up, I told him what I had discovered and asked him to leave and never return.

When the customer came to pick up his "free" work later that day, I learned my manager had been trading lab services for his professional expertise that was—at least in part—benefitting our business. Unfortunately, the day manager had not shared this arrangement with me nor asked my approval, so I bought into the scenario the evening manager had painted. And I regretted my hasty actions and wished I had looked into the matter before firing my employee.

The lesson I learned through this experience was costly to everyone. And from that day forward I have tried to fully examine a matter and spend more time in prayer before making a major decision.

A little later, I hired a knowledgeable young showroom manager. He was very capable and a good photographer in his own right. He could satisfy any customer with constructive ways of improving their photography. I put my trust in him, giving him a key to the showroom so he could come in early to be ready for customers.

Since we counted inventory only once a year back then, we had no way of balancing sales with inventory. If supplies were dwindling, we ordered more. However, I began noticing that our inventory was shrinking far more quickly than usual. Then one day, the young manager failed to show up to work. That very same day, a regular customer who lived a distance away came in to confess that he was receiving goods at excellent prices delivered to his business at night in our delivery van (usually parked at the store off hours). He had finally pieced together that my manager was scamming me, and he had come in that day to make restitution for the off-book deliveries.

We never saw that showroom manager again. However, the police caught up with him. While they were making a case against him, he fled to California. We estimated our loss at $40,000.

From this escapade, I learned once again that more supervision is better than less. I became vigilant with our property. But I also continued to put my trust in God, who is altogether trustworthy.

And God faithfully advanced the business.

Collections: Cameras, Photographs and "Sebastians"

I've always loved cameras of all shapes, sizes and models. My friends gave me their outdated cameras and I purchased antiques at flea markets. My camera collection grew from year to year. When I had accumulated over 700 cameras and photo accessories I decided to sell most of the collection to a neighbor, John Long, a retired industrial arts teacher and good friend—a nicer guy you've

My original camera collection was dearly loved and
gave me great joy as I added new finds from time to time;
this was a small snapshot of the whole.

never met. Though John and some of his retired education associates had dreamed of one day opening a museum, I believe the cameras are still in boxes.

In addition to the antique cameras I kept, my basement holds several other unofficial collections. One of those is a vast assortment of prints, photographs and slides I have taken over the past 80 years.

Jean and I love visiting beautiful places like the New England states, east coast beaches, and Colonial Williamsburg. Williamsburg boasts excellent architecture and portrays colonial life with costumed re-enactors. I have enjoyed taking pictures in these places and cherish my collection of 16"x20" salon prints.

Dad enjoyed taking a trip with us to Williamsburg where I appropriately captured him in this photo, pulling on the blacksmith's bellows and gripping a hammer on the anvil.

I believe it was the summer of 1958 when Jean and I vacationed in the Boston area and first saw small figurines called Sebastian Miniatures. We bought a darling three-inch-tall rendering of a little fisherman clutching a large fish, thus starting a new collection we would enjoy building for many years. The clerk told us Sebastian Miniatures were made by artist Prescott Baston in Marblehead, an old seaport east of Boston. We wanted to know more about these figures that carried our name, so we investigated the area to see if could find Mr. Baston and his studio.

Marblehead is a lovely harbor town. Traveling around its narrow streets we found the Sebastian Studio. Entering the small wooden two-story building, I asked to see Mr. Baston.

The young woman managing the first-floor giftshop greeted us and said she would tell the artist we were there. She returned and said, "Mr. Baston can't see you today. He's pouring plaster."

Disappointed we did not have time to wait, we decided we would try to return to Massachusetts the following year on our vacation.

The next summer we met the dear old artist, his wife, and his son Woody and family. Woody had studied art at Boston College and spent a number of years as an officer in the US Army serving in Italy where he enjoyed studying the great sculptures of the masters. Like his dad, Woody was starting to create Sebastian Miniatures.

Prescott had begun this line in 1948 with historical figures of famous people and depictions of life along the coast of New England. Jean and I became more and more interested in Sebastians in the late '70s. With more than 2,000 active collectors, the Bastons urged us to publish a newsletter that covered their

The four Sebastian Miniatures on the left were produced for our Sebastian Exchange members; the covered wagon on the right commemorated a Lancaster Bible College anniversary.

current figurines and an aftermarket report and value register of the older Sebastians. We took on the task...and a task it was! I photographed every piece — hundreds — and researched their values. I worked on gathering interesting information and putting together quality newsletters, gaining my daughter Nancy's help as I taught her how to write, edit, create layout boards for the printer, and more creative tasks.

Every June, a Sebastian Miniatures festival was held in the Boston area. We called our newsletter *The Sebastian Exchange* and occupied a display booth alongside the many dealers who sold Sebastians at the yearly festival. One the most fascinating features of this event was the look-a-like contest. Collectors would dress-up like one of the Sebastian Miniature figurines. Nancy entered the contest many years; the first time, she portrayed the Chiquita Banana lady and ended up over 8' tall. One year, she dressed as "Mrs. Rittenhouse Square," a Philadelphia socialite viewing a bust of Ben Franklin in a museum. I wish you could have seen the finished entry, for which she won the grand prize!

Nancy worked with me on our publications for eight years, and then took over the work almost completely. To shorten a lengthy story, I will just say that the number of collectors decreased over that next ten years making it unfeasible to continue the Sebastian Exchange Collectors Society. It had been great fun, and I mark this as the beginning of Nancy's writing success as a nationally published author in the traditional print market.

And so, the final collection in my basement is very "Sebastian" — comprised of 758 (at last count) Sebastian Miniatures, past issues of *The Sebastian Exchange* newsletters, and mountains of prints, slides and layout materials from years of publishing. Oh, and some costume pieces still exist. Great fun!

I am fascinated to see how God perfectly placed together so many aspects of photography and design in my life plan.

Chapter 8

Family

T he first 13 years of our marriage were busy, happy times for Jean and me, even though we were a bit disappointed that God did not bless us with children. It was very challenging to trust God in this area.

Jean and I are posing in our backyard in the early '60s.

Josie, Mom and Dad often visited our home on Pine Drive.

While Jean continued to manage the business aspects of the Hirt company, I served our customers, attended training sessions provided by our vendors, and called on clients with our factory representatives, all the while teaching missions courses, attending faculty meetings, and continuing to design buildings for LSB.

Sunday evenings, the Gospel Center quartet often sang before the message and movie, on the municipal airport grounds.

I also served on the Deacon Board of The Gospel Center. During this time the Gospel Center started a "Drive-in Church" located at the abandoned Lancaster Airport (where the High Steel sales building is now located, behind Red Rose Commons Mall). We built a 30' square movie screen and used a powerful 16mm arc projector to show Christian films after every Sunday night message during the summer months.

A Surprise!

In the spring of 1961, Jean went to the hospital for an ectopic operation. I impatiently waited for the doctor's report. After what seemed like an eternity, he finally called me into Jean's hospital room when she returned from recovery.

The doctor looked rather sheepish and announced, "There was no problem. It's a baby. Congratulations!"

We could hardly believe we were finally going to be parents. The long wait had somewhat numbed our hopes and disappointment. To say the doctor's news surprised us would have been an understatement of great proportion.

Wanting everything to be just right for our little child, we began making plans for his or her future. Our church offered a very small Sunday School with various ages in a single class. We thought it best to join a Bible church with a larger, well-organized Sunday School program for our child. We chose Calvary Independent Church (now Calvary Church on the Landis Valley Road) and felt right at home since we had attended Calvary missions conferences for many years, as far back as our Penn State days. Dr. Frank Torry was the senior pastor, and I had come to know him personally because of his intense interest in photography and Leica cameras.

On September 17, 1961, Jean and I were blessed with a darling baby girl. We named her Nancy Jean: Nancy because we wanted her to be a friendly person with a love for people, and Jean to honor her mother. (Nancy was also the name of Jean's favorite childhood paper dolls and the name of my sister's largest doll.)

One July evening when Nancy was four, we stopped to pick her up at Jean's parents' home after work (they often babysat for us). Martin told us how they had taken her with them to an evangelistic meeting being held at their church. When visiting evangelist, Dr. Orr, gave the invitation, Nancy had tried to push by her grandfather to go forward, but he would not let her pass, thinking she was too young to understand the invitation.

The Esbenshades told us that dear Nancy had sat down in her seat and wept silent tears, continuing to cry for some time after the service. Pastor Stoll had come down the aisle and stopped to ask Nancy why she was crying. When she told him she wanted to be saved, he had immediately knelt down with her and helped her pray to accept Christ as her Savior.

When Jean and I returned home with her, Nancy wanted to tell us the whole story. We rejoiced that our precious little daughter had invited Jesus into her heart.

Nancy received a wonderful education and rich Biblical foundation at Lancaster Christian School from kindergarten through eighth grade. Then she enjoyed four years at Conestoga Valley High School (CVHS). Very active in the

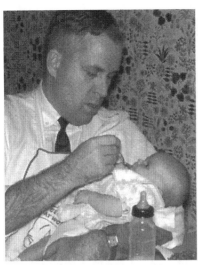

I enjoyed feeding Nancy (left), and she always smiled her thanks (above).

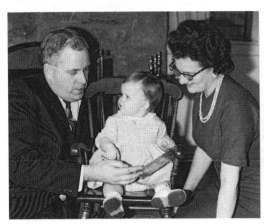

Nancy and I have an equal delight for good food.

Jean and I loved reading books to our little daughter.

My bachelor cousin Richard (the pilot) loved holding little Nancy. (left)

Just prior to Uncle Walther's passing, he held his great niece. (below)

One of my favorite photos of Nancy,
in her dandelion garden

high school music program, she played the flute and piccolo in the concert and marching bands. Marching at football games was exciting for the band and the fans!

Each year I shot tons of pictures of the CVHS band on Kodachrome slides, from which I put together slide shows with Boston Pops marches as background music. Students and parents enjoyed the entertaining show at the end-of-the-year music banquet. For the ninth-grade project, I used two slide projectors and a dissolve unit. By Nancy's senior year, I had graduated to showcasing the band, chorus and orchestra on three screens, utilizing six slide projectors and a movie projector. It seemed like every kid in the school—and all their family—turned out for that final show. What great fun it was!

Tim Grove, Jean's nephew, also participated in the music programs at CVHS several years after Nancy. We got to enjoy the marching band and concerts all over again. And I put on similar end-of-year shows for Tim and his classmates. Tim went on to study communications and history at Messiah College and American History at George Mason University. Today Tim is Chief of Museum Learning at the Smithsonian's National Air and Space Museum, as well as an author and educator.

Although Jean and I worked hard in business and ministry, almost every year we took a family vacation to Camp of the Woods on Lake Pleasant in

Nancy and I have wonderful memories of family trips to Colonial Williamsburg, Virginia.

Speculator, New York. Their motto is "Vacation on Purpose." That was the place to go with our family—Nancy, Jean and me, and later, with our grand-daughter, Becky.

We originally heard about the camp when Jean's sister Kathy was dating a staffer shortly after we got married. Later when Nancy came along, we wanted a family-oriented vacation environment where we could return year after year and create lasting family memories.

We thoroughly enjoy the great Bible teaching in morning chapel services, wonderful fellowship with other believers, spectacular concerts, good food and the delicious mountain air. Year after year, for more than 55 years, we keep going back.

Nancy went on to study elementary education at Lancaster Bible College and Millersville University, received her Master's in Education from East Stroudsburg University, and taught for many years as a classroom teacher and substitute. She has also written several nationally published books and encourages women through an inspirational speaking ministry. I am so grateful she has helped me edit and arrange this collection of stories.

Like Jean and me, Nancy and her first husband had just one daughter. Our granddaughter, Becky, graduated from Conestoga Valley High School with a scholarship to Wilkes University but—to our delight—finished at Lancaster Bible College in 2014, giving us three generations of LBC graduates. Today she is in management at United Parcel Service (UPS) and delights us with frequent visits.

The adventures we have enjoyed with both Nancy and Becky would fill volumes of books. Suffice it to say, Jean and I adore our girls!

Becky graduated from CVHS (left) and—much to my delight—LBC (right), making three generations of LBC graduates: Paul 1952, Nancy 1984, and Becky 2014.

Jean's Large Extended Family

Although my immediate family is small, Jean has a large extended family. Her mother's name was Brubaker; her father was an Esbenshade. Both families were large: Jean's mother had nine siblings, and her father had two sisters and four brothers. Grandpa Brubaker was the pastor of the Strasburg Mennonite Church for many years. Typical for Mennonite preachers of the time, he was a working farmer. Jean's uncles all had large families, and her cousins were many. In the early years, it was rather difficult to remember all the names. But as I got to know relatives on a personal basis, the task grew easier. I was well accepted by the whole family.

At Christmastime, Grandma Brubaker traditionally invited the entire family for dinner. The typical Mennonite family meal was prepared by Grandma and all of her daughters and daughters-in-law. When I began dating Jean, I experienced my first Christmas dinner with Grandma. It was 1947, the year after Grandpa passed away (I never had the privilege of meeting him). Grandma's home was spacious, but with the whole clan present—well over 50 adults and children—the house was stuffed. Since no table could accommodate all of us, three tables were set. The adults sat together and the kids had their own area.

A mouth-watering aroma greeted every person who stepped in the door. The meal began with silence descending, and the eldest brother asked God's blessing on the food. As with the typical Mennonite meal (I learned), we enjoyed five different meats, no end of vegetables, fluffy whipped potatoes, hot gravy, bread and jam...so delicious! Platters kept circulating until no one could eat another bite.

After the main course, dishes were cleared to make room for dessert. Cracker pudding, made with saltine crackers and coconut, was served as a transition between the meal and sweets. Then the ladies brought in a variety of desserts. That pudding course was new to me; in fact, I had never tasted cracker pudding and found it delightful (see Grandma's recipe in Appendix C).

When the meal was finished, everyone was again silent. We all bowed our heads for a moment of thanks to God, and then we thanked the women who had prepared the meal. A short musical program followed. I was noted as a soloist in those days; when I was asked to sing, I experienced a grand feeling of acceptance. I remember Uncle Harry, direct and outspoken, saying to me, "That was good Paul. You sing like we do, but you pronounce your words a little differently." I guess that made sense, since I was from Philadelphia.

Jean's Brubaker uncles impressed me. Uncle Ara was a lawyer in Florida and Uncle Earl was an executive of Borden Foods, a national food company based in New York City – both had attended universities. Uncle Lester was a dealer for Allis-Chalmers farm implements, and his younger brother Roy operated a branch division in Lititz. John, Jay and Harry were farmers. Jean had two aunts as well, Mabel and May.

One day, Jean and I were invited to Uncle Lester and Aunt Ada's home to make donuts. You could smell the donuts cooking before you even walked into the house. Donut perfume...lovely! Three or four pots of boiling oil occupied the cooktop, and the ladies in the kitchen mixed donut batter and dropped it by spoonfuls into the hot grease. From the pot, we took out the donuts and topped them with powdered sugar, granular sugar, cinnamon, or glaze. We enjoyed hot donuts right off the cooling racks (I am sure I ate too many). By the end of the afternoon, dozens and dozens of donuts were packaged for family, friends and neighbors.

I was accepted as part of the family on every occasion, and to this day we all enjoy a lively Brubaker reunion in June, currently planned by the grandchildren of Christian and Fannie Brubaker, Jean's maternal grandparents.

Jean's paternal grandparents, the Esbenshades, were older and did not do nearly as much entertaining as the Brubakers. Grandpa was a farmer all his life. He enjoyed Grandma's good cooking and had the tummy to prove it. I have a mental picture of him sitting in the living room with his little dog perched on what little lap he could provide.

I remember one meal with the whole Esbenshade family: several uncles, two aunts, and bushel of cousins. The dinner was primarily turkey, and Grandma made delicious filling with oysters — quite a delicacy. As we headed to Grandma's that morning, Jean had tried to warn me that the uncles would get into heated arguments about who's farming techniques were best, often parting with unsettled feelings, a reality I witnessed later that day.

I came to love and appreciate Jean's huge family. The love and compassion I witnessed often over the years helped me picture the family and home life I wanted to build with Jean.

My Sister-in-Law

Jean had only one sister, Kathy. Mother Esbenshade had given birth to a stillborn son between Jean and Kathy. This situation reminded me of my own family, in which the son between Josie and me had passed away at an early age.

Kathy was ten years younger than me, and I teased her as if she was my own little sister. She would sit across from me at meals in Mom's kitchen and not eat much. I would often say, "You have the appetite of a bird."

She would push the remainder of her dinner over to me. When I ate it — and I always did — she would giggle and call me a bottomless pit.

One very hot July day after Jean and I married and moved to the farm in Lancaster, I was outside washing the car. Noticing that Kathy sat on the stoop watching, I called to her, "Would you please bring me a drink of water?"

She ran into the house and came out again with an insulated aluminum glass. I thought this was great. It would keep the ice from melting for a while. I put down the hose and thanked her. As I took a huge gulp of *very hot water*, I realized I had been duped.

She giggled and called as she ran off, "That's what you get for teasing me!"

During her senior year at Manheim Township High School, Kathy often visited Jean at Penn State, hoping to attend there after graduation. On one such visit she stayed overnight in the dorm. During a surprise inspection by the resident assistant, Jean and her roommate hid Kathy in a closet where she was not discovered. She was very

Jean's sister Kathryn (Kathy) celebrated her fifteenth birthday while we were living at the farmhouse.

Kathy and her husband Orie were blessed with a wonderful son, Tim Grove, in 1967 (above). Tim is shown again with Nancy (top right) at the Esbenshade home, and with his family (right) during his high school years.

quiet by nature but loved that exciting adventure!

Kathy spent two years at Penn State, then transferred to Barrington Bible College in Rhode Island. After graduation, she was awarded a secretarial position with IVCF in their Philadelphia office. Enjoying the attentions of several suitors over the years, she finally met and fell in love with Orie Grove. Orie, a handsome gentleman from Hershey, PA, was an engineer working for duPont and a fine Christian young man. We were all so happy for her.

Kathy and Orie enjoyed a good life here in Lancaster and raised one son, Tim. Kathy passed away in her early '80s after several years of Alzheimer's. We loved her dearly and miss her very much.

A Word from Nephew Tim Grove

As an historian, educator and author (and Paul's only nephew), I have hoped for many years that we would somehow manage to record some of Uncle Paul's amazing life—not just for its window into the changing world around us, but for its window into abiding faith amidst that change. I work to teach the lessons of the past to literally millions of people who view the exhibitions I've developed, and I know it's the personal stories that resonate longest with most people. I'm thrilled that Uncle Paul has taken

Tim Grove

the time to write his stories and is willing to share them in a book. We all have a responsibility to share God's faithfulness with future generations. To quote the Song of Moses from Deuteronomy chapter 32, verse 7: "Remember the days of old; consider the generations long past. Ask your father and he will tell you, your elders, and they will explain to you." We all have stories that serve as examples to future generations. Uncle Paul has been a big influence in my life, and I'm thankful that God continues to use him in big and small ways.

Sister Josie

I mentioned my sister Josie in the early chapters of this book. A short time after graduation from Beaver College, Josie taught music at Upper Moreland High School. She was hired to fill Mr. Headly's position when he was drafted into the Army. After the war, he returned to his job.

During her time teaching at the high school, Josie experienced problems with her voice. A specialist unsuccessfully removed nodules on her vocal chords, damaging her vocal musculature in the process. As her voice healed, she realized she was no longer a soprano but a weak alto...permanently. As her teaching job came to an end — and with the crushing blow of losing her singing voice — she needed to rethink her life plans.

Mother and Dad suggested she go back to school and study to become a secretary and work in an office setting. She did so, and later secured a position with J.E. Caldwell and Co. Jewelers in downtown Philadelphia, where she met

Josie's remditions of hymns and faorite songs often led us in evenings of family singing in the Nash-Everett home. (above)

Mom and Dad entertained in grand style in the dining room I designed for them. (right)

Visits with extended family was always a treat. In the photo above, Dad and I are sitting with Uncle Armon Gruel who recommended me for the job I got with duPont after high school. Below, my aunts Lillie and Jenny are enjoying one of Mom's sumptuous dinners.

My cousin George and I spent great times together, even in our later years. (right)

Peter Sebastian (George's son) married Polly (right), shown here with their daughter Anna (left), and son Barry and his wife Mindy on their wedding day. (below)

Maxwell Aronow. We all came to love Max, a man several years older than Josie who treated her very well. Max enjoyed visiting us in Lancaster.

When Max passed away, Josie moved to Lancaster to live with and care for Dad. She taught private voice and piano lessons and enjoyed her pet dogs. Josie passed away at the age of 78.

Cousin George

My cousin George served in the US Navy in World War II as an officer on a cruiser in the Pacific Ocean. His ship was torpedoed by the Japanese, and he spent several hours in the water before being rescued. He was sent to New York City with his cruiser which underwent repairs at the Brooklyn Naval Yard. He regained his strength in a hospital where he met and fell in love with his nurse, Eleanor Barton. George and Eleanor married and expanded their family by two children, Sally and Peter, as well as many grandchildren and now great-grandchildren. George went to Heaven in 2000, and Eleanor joined him last year in 2016.

Chapter 9

Retirement

Even though I do not yet consider myself to be fully retired, I began the process of downsizing my business interests in the early '90s, selling the photo lab to friend and colleague Bob Wiker. Then after years of fruitless searching for a buyer for HIRTECH, Jean and I gratefully passed on the photo business to Dennis Fahnestock. Finally, ten years ago, I sold my Sebastian Darkroom Products business to Jim Carr from California Stainless — however, I continue to design and create products as a consultant.

Am I retired? Mostly, I guess. Work keeps me feeling like I have purpose. But I fill the rest of my time with the things I love: photography, Lancaster Bible College, family and my faith. How I praise God for the opportunity to enjoy all of this, yet still actively serve Him.

Photography

Like most industries, photography changes. The biggest change happened when film and paper gave way to digital images. In George Eastman's days, a photographer coated glass plates before capturing an image inside a camera. Wet plates were replaced by a dry process. Then he introduced a small hand camera with a roll of paper that could produce 100 prints. Still later, he created film that could be developed into negatives for making reprints. Polaroid gave us prints almost immediately, right out of the camera, even in color. In today's computer age, images are recorded on tiny electronic chips. Everyone has a camera built into their ever-present phone, with no worry about running out of film (although memory might be an issue). And we can send high quality images around the world with the tap of a finger. Amazing!

The teaching of wet photography has disappeared from most high schools today, but it is still very popular as a classic art form in universities and art schools. The extreme attraction of wet photography courses quite often creates long waiting lists of art students.

I continuously enjoy the privilege of designing facilities and equipment to furnish state-of-the-art photo darkrooms. These facilities are a far cry from my early days of darkroom exploration in the cellar of Cousin George's farmhouse.

This 1950s shot of the square in Lancaster includes the famous soldiers' monument that is still there today.

Today I also enjoy taking pictures with a digital camera and looking at my photos on my computer. The convenience, economy, and versatility of digital photography never ceases to amaze me. I wonder what is coming next...

As mentioned several times in earlier chapters, looking through photos to accompany my narrative has been a daunting but fun challenge. I chose to include here a few additional pictures; they may not fit a particular story but are interesting in their own right. Photography captures special moments, as well as showing us how time changes things. I hope you enjoy these glimpses into history.

I assume this is the most famous person I have ever photographed. I used a 4"x5" Crown Graphic camera with a 180mm Zeiss Sonar lens while jostled by the huge throng in front of the Fulton Bank building in 1960 when John F. Kennedy campaigned through center city Lancaster.

The Amish people add local color to Lancaster County.

Jean and I have always loved the Jersey shore,
where these photos were shot in the early 50s; Ocean City (left)
and Atlantic City (above) with the Steel Pier
where we saw the lady on the diving horse.

Compare
these photos
of our home
on Pine Drive.
We moved in on
Thanksgiving Day
1955, when our
front oak tree
was 1.5" in
diameter (top).
Today (bottom),
its truck is
40" across and
we have enjoyed
every moment
of its growth—
and ours.

Lancaster Bible College

Nothing but my family pleases me more than the continued growth of LBC.

It is always a privilege to spend time with my cherished friend and president of the college, Dr. Peter Teague. I know him to be a strong and gracious leader who walks with God.

I love to read Peter's updates and to drive around the campus to witness the progress. I also still enjoy serving on the Board of Trustees, Building Committee and Corporation.

Through the ups and downs, LBC's spiritual values and academic goals have remained constant over the years, for which I am so very grateful. At LBC, God is worshipped and glorified, and His Word is fully and faithfully taught. The student body has grown from 35 students in a downtown Lancaster building during my freshman year to over 2,000 students at five locations and online today. LBC is a premier learning community, intentionally developing the head, heart and hand of servant ministry leaders, and impacting our world to the glory of God. This blesses my soul.

In my remaining years, I hope there is more for me to do at the college.

Jim Fetterolf, My Friend

One of my dearest also-retired friends, Jim Fetterolf, serves with me at LBC. He is the secretary of the Board of Trustees. I love his salvation story. As a young boy, he was left alone on the farm one day while his mother and dad went to town. His forbidden sport of choice was riding the pigs! Once his parents were down the lane and out of sight that day, he jumped on a pig. Unfortunately for him, they forgot something and turned around to retrieve it, finding him enjoying his sport. His punishment was going to Sunday School—where he found Jesus Christ as his Savior. Shortly thereafter, his one-room schoolhouse burned to the ground, and he was moved to a different school where he met his lifelong sweetheart, Rhoda. Today Jim and Rhoda are precious friends to Jean and me, and we frequently enjoy dinner and activities with them.

My Wife

As much as it will pain dearest Jeanne to be highlighted even so briefly, I must mention her as I close. I would not be the man I am today, nor would I have been able to accomplish so very much to God's glory, were it not for this faithful, loving and honorable wife. Proverbs 31 is accurate in saying a good wife is more valuable than rubies.

I am so thankful for my dear wife, and very, very grateful we are still together, celebrating our sixty-ninth wedding anniversary in 2017. The Lord richly poured out His blessing upon me when He brought us together. Jean has made my life richer in so many ways and is a treasure I cherish more than life itself.

We worked together in the photo business for many years. As my bookkeeper, Jean paid the bills, processed billing, paid our staff and did mundane details that freed me to work with people and grow the business.

Jean is such a delight to me—and very beautiful! A quiet and retiring person, she is not truly known by many people. Therefore, let me share just a few of the things that make her unique, so you can get a personal glimpse of the love of my life.

She is a true friend who has never disappointed me. God gifted Jean with wisdom to help me in all my decisions. She possesses a solid understanding of Biblical doctrine, thanks to Dr. Henry Heydt, her pastor for many years. Whatever problems we have faced, Jean has always been there with the encouragement I needed. I am so very thankful God saved her just for me.

Jean posed for this lovely portrait in the 2005, complete with flowers.

Together we have enjoyed the growth of our dear daughter and granddaughter through the years. We always look forward to trips with Nancy and Becky. And we feel honored when they seek us out for discussions and prayer during difficulties—or celebrate victories with us.

We do enjoy traveling, eating out in restaurants, and reading together. But while I work, Jean has several hobbies that she enjoys alone. She is a wonderful gardener and homemaker. Our house in the spring and summer is surrounded by beautiful flowers that remind me of traditional English gardens.

She cuts fresh flowers to bring in and arrange throughout our house during the growing months. Our home is beautiful, too. It is always clean, neat and so comfortable. I am grateful beyond words to be so well cared for.

Jean makes our home a delightful refuge from the world.

Jean, an excellent cook and baker, has provided hospitality to countless missionaries in our home over the years. While I have collected cameras and other things, Jean has amassed a collection of cookbooks. I have included a few of her best recipes (my favorites) in Appendix D.

As it says in Song of Solomon 3:4, "I found the one I love."

Jean and I celebrated our 65th wedding anniversary in this photo taken at Longwood Gardens; this year will be 69.

The Bible

I wish to end my memories with this account, for more than anything else I believe it has changed me—even now at the end of my life—into a better man.

About five years ago, while my granddaughter Becky was attending LBC, she stopped by the house and sat with me for several minutes in the living room. I remember her asking, "Grandpa, did you ever read all the way through the Bible from beginning to end?"

Now that you know the history behind my poor reading skills, you will understand why I answered in the negative. "Well, Becky, I'm always reading the Bible, but only sections of it, particularly what applies to my need. I've always used the Word of God to guide me. But I've never read the Bible completely from Genesis to Revelation." I thought a minute and added, "Your grandmother and I read some of God's Word every morning and pray together."

Over the next several days, the Holy Spirit used Becky's question to convict and challenge me to read the Word, cover to cover. I thought, I can do this!

I began reading.

Today I am still reading. I have read through the Bible three times, and I am now studying book-by-book through the New Testament.

Something else I have done in semi-retirement has to do with prayer. I built a prayer list and I use it daily to remember my family, friends, some of whom are unsaved, missionaries, LBC and other ministries and their particular needs. The prayer list changes weekly because of the ease with which I can use the computer to update and reprint it. It gives me great joy to remember dear ones to the Lord, and then contact them to see how God is working in their lives. How wonderful to see His answers.

Of all the things I have done that I would encourage you to do also, nothing is as important as *reading God's Word and praying*. I urge you to do it. You will be blessed now and forever.

Concluding Thoughts and Lessons Learned

ecently I was privileged to listen to a great Bible teacher as he spoke on worshipping God. "In worship," he said, "we need to remember the Holy Moments God puts along our path and praise Him for His love and faithfulness." In taking up his challenge and while writing this history, I have recalled many of those times when God touched my life and directed me along the path He designed for me.

My Holy Moments

1. God placed me in a Christian home with loving parents.

2. God gave me a fine Christian missionary-sending church where I received Christ as my personal Savior and committed my life to serve Him.

3. God led me safely through World War II and saw that I met and worked with a missionary in China.

4. God led me to Penn State's InterVarsity Christian Fellowship where I met Jean, the love of my life; where I met Dr. Heydt, my godly mentor and personal friend; where I first met my best friend Don DeHart and also Martin and Anna Esbenshade, Jean's Mom and Dad, whom I admired and loved dearly.

5. God gave me His choice, Jean, as my lovely wife of now 69 years, and He gave me a cherished daughter, Nancy, and wonderful grand-daughter, Becky. I'm so pleased that Nancy, Becky and I are all grad-uates of LBC.

6. God led me to Lancaster School of the Bible where Dr. Heydt invited me to serve on the Board of Directors of EGM/UFM/Crossworld for over 50 years

7. God allowed me to teach courses for students who were preparing for missionary service. As China closed its doors to missionary work, LBC

was God's new direction for me, including the privilege of helping to develop a new campus over the next 60 years.

8. God introduced me to Oscar H. Hirt, who I joined in business and with whom I served on the BCM Board of Directors for almost 40 years.

9. God gave me the privilege of personally knowing and working with all five LBC presidents; and though semi-retired, I continue to serve the Lord with the LBC Trustees in my 42nd year.

10. God has given me many opportunities over the years to invent, design, create, write and do business in ways that help others, provide for my family's needs, bring me great joy and reflect my Creator's image (hopefully bringing Him glory).

11. God has given me — in my golden years — a great love for His Word and a passion for connecting with Him through prayer, interceding for many loved ones and missionaries.

My Life Lessons

In writing this account of my life, I have been encouraged by those who hear about the project to conclude with the major lessons God has taught me over the course of my lifetime. I wish you could read, learn and apply these lessons to your own life without going through the difficult circumstances it often takes for us to grow and mature.

These are the lessons I have learned…and am learning.

1. Jesus Christ's gift of eternal salvation gives life…now!
   Accept Him as your Savior.

2. God's way is always the best way; He has a plan.
   Trust Him.

3. God will direct us, if we ask and are willing to obey.
   Follow Him.

4. God always equips us for the tasks He assigns.
   Use His resources.

5. There is no substitute for reading God's Word.
   Read every day.

6. Prayer gives us comfort, confidence and compassion for people.
   Pray regularly.

7. God hears and answers our prayers according to His Will.
   Pray according to the Scriptures.

8. People matter more than tasks or things.
   Love people.

9. Situations must be investigated carefully before confronting people.
   Listen and research thoroughly.

10. Slow and steady wins the race (as we trust God).
    Persevere with patience.

11. God has given us a great many things to enjoy.
    Give thanks.

In Conclusion

Thank you for taking the time to read this history of my life as I remember it. I close with the following words from one of my favorite hymns and some beloved Scripture verses.

All the way my Savior leads me; what have I to ask beside?
Can I doubt His tender mercy, who through life has been my Guide?
Heavenly peace, divinest comfort, here by faith in Him to dwell!
For I know, whate'er befall me, Jesus doeth all things well.

All the way my Savior leads me, oh, the fullness of His love!
Perfect rest to me is promised, in my Father's house above.
When my spirit, clothed immortal, wings its flight to realms of day,
This my song through endless ages: Jesus led me all the way.

— Fannie Crosby

"I will bless the LORD at all times; His praise shall continually be in my mouth." (Psalm 34:1)

"Delight yourself also in the LORD, and He shall give you the desires of your heart." (Psalm 37:4)

"I love the LORD, because He has heard my voice and my supplications. Because He has inclined His ear to me, therefore I will call upon Him as long as I live." (Psalm 116:1, 2)

"Your word I have hidden in my heart, that I might not sin against You." (Psalm 119:11)

"Trust in the LORD with all your heart, and lean not on your own understanding; in all your ways acknowledge Him, and He shall direct your paths." (Proverbs 3:5-6)

"A man's heart plans his way, but the LORD directs his steps." (Proverbs 16:9)

"The grass withers, the flower fades, but the word of our God stands forever." (Isaiah 40:8)

"For God so loved the world that He gave His only begotten Son, that whoever believes in Him should not perish but have everlasting life." (John 3:16)

"I beseech you therefore, brethren, by the mercies of God, that you present your bodies a living sacrifice, holy, acceptable to God, which is your reasonable service. And do not be

conformed to this world, but be transformed by the renewing of your mind, that you may prove what is that good and acceptable and perfect will of God." (Romans 12:1-2)

"I have been crucified with Christ; it is no longer I who live, but Christ lives in me; and the life which I now live in the flesh I live by faith in the Son of God, who loved me and gave Himself for me." (Galatians 2:20)

"For by grace you have been saved through faith, and that not of yourselves; it is the gift of God, not of works, lest anyone should boast." (Ephesians 2:8-9)

"He who calls you is faithful, who also will do it." (I Thessalonians 5:24)

Nancy's Afterword

Not many men in the world today have led such an excellent life and live to write about it. With Paul J. Sebastian, this is not a boast but reality, which he humbly credits to God. I know. I am his daughter.

Dad may be the oldest engineer still designing today. His name graces a building at Lancaster Bible College where he has served for over 60 years. At over 90, he still looks about 75. Yet I often find Dad sitting at his desk or in his living room chair reading his Bible and praying over his prayer list. He is a humble man, and I am proud to call him my father.

I loved growing up with a creative dad. I went to him most often for help with major school projects. The first thing we made together for an early grade school assignment was a stuffed aardvark. Later projects included models of the Jewish Temple, Joan of Arc, and the Solar System. As I got older, we even won prizes for our creative efforts. He did not demand perfection from me, but his excellence motivated me to do my very best, then and now.

Although he generously met my every need, Dad did not lavish too much attention or too many gifts on me as some fathers of only children would or could. From what you read about his involvement in missions, church and LBC, you know he gave extensively of his time, effort and means to things beyond me. This helped me grow up without a sense of entitlement. In fact, Dad was so busy that vacations were one of my favorite times to connect with him. He made our summer trek to Camp of the Woods a yearly priority and spent lots of time with me in that relaxed setting.

Rainy days at Camp found Dad and me in the craft room. People would walk by the table where he was creating a work of art and say, "Oh, would you look at that!" I just about busted my buttons with pride in him. One year when I was in grade school, he and I collected our finished projects on Friday morning and went directly to the dining hall for lunch. Waiting for Mom and for the doors to open, an adult camper noticed Dad's project and exclaimed, "Art must be your dad's hobby!" When I enthusiastically agreed, she said, "What's your mother's hobby?"

Since I had never considered Mom in terms of a hobby, I thought about what I saw my mother doing at home most of the time and finally answered "cleaning." This earned a chuckle from the group waiting with us. Dad and I have teased Mom about it ever since. As I grew older, though, I learned the importance of my mother's homemaking skills in Dad's life. And I have appreciated the unique partnership they share, fueled by the love God designed just for them.

Of all the things that impress me about my father, probably the greatest is his generosity. For example, his missions giving extends far beyond the Sunday offering plate. As a youngster, I did not understand why missionaries who visited our home would shake Dad's hand and then hug him or shake again...until as I grew older I realized he was slipping them cash on their way out our door. I have seen him call a waitress over and pay the check for ministry friends at a separate table who happened to be in the same restaurant at the same time. And I know he gives far more in other ways—more than I know of—whenever a need arises and God prompts him. I am so thankful for his huge heart and his willingness to listen to God and share.

Who Dad is and what he has done give testimony to God's presence and work in his life. I believe Psalm 112 best encapsulates Dad's life with these words:

> *Praise the Lord!*
> *Blessed is the man who fears the Lord,*
> *Who delights greatly in His commandments.*
> *His descendants will be mighty on earth;*
> *The generation of the upright will be blessed.*
> *Wealth and riches will be in his house,*
> *And his righteousness endures forever.*
> *Unto the upright there arises light in the darkness;*
> *He is gracious, and full of compassion, and righteous.*
> *A good man deals graciously and lends;*
> *He will guide his affairs with discretion.*
> *Surely he will never be shaken;*
> *The righteous will be in everlasting remembrance.*
> *He will not be afraid of evil tidings;*
> *His heart is steadfast, trusting in the Lord.*
> *His heart is established;*
> *He will not be afraid,*
> *Until he sees his desire upon his enemies.*
> *He has dispersed abroad,*
> *He has given to the poor;*
> *His righteousness endures forever;*
> *His horn will be exalted with honor.*

Nancy Sebastian Kuch, M.Ed.

Appendix A

Timeline

Sebastian Family History, prior to Paul

1500s First known Sebastian ancestors live in Spain

1600s Family flees to Germany under religious persecution

1700s Sons marry German brides and move to Alsace-Lorraine, then America

1800s Historical discrepancies with family name: Sebastian to Bastian to Sebastian

1844 George Byards Bastian (Paul's grandfather) is born in Zelienople, PA

1893 James Endres (Paul's father) is born to George and Carolyn Bastian in Williamsport, PA

1895 Mary Viola (Paul's mother) is born to Harry and Viola Coeyman in Hatboro, PA

1905 James moves in with his brother Walter's family in Churchville, PA

1914 James and Mary marry in Philadelphia

1915 Mary Josephine (Paul's sister) is born

1919 James Enders Jr. (Paul's brother) is born

1923 James Jr. dies at age four during the worldwide influenza epidemic

Paul's History

1924 Paul Judson Sebastian is born on January 4

1925 Jean Esbenshade is born on July 30 (becomes Paul's wife at age 23)

1929 Begins Elementary School
Stock Market Crash; Great Depression Begins

1930 Creates first Architectural Drawing

1931 Views father installing the North Transept Rose Window in the National Cathedral

1934 Begins designing and building bunks (outdoor playhouses)

1936   Becomes "striker" in dad's blacksmith shop
       Decides on life of drawing, design and engineering

1937   Salvation experience (February 7)
       First lessons in photography from Cousin George (summer)
       Begins odd jobs and inventions (junior high and high school)

1938   Baptism and dedication of his life to God's service

1939   *World War II Begins (September 1)*
       Begins sports reporting and photo journalism

1940   Employed by surveyor; math class with professional engineer/teacher
       Teaches Sunday School class of 12-year-old boys

1941   Graduates from Upper Moreland High School in Willow Grove (June)
       Graduates from Mastbaum Vocational School in Mechanical Drawing (3
           months)
       Works in Engineering Department of the duPont Company in
           Wilmington, DE

1942   Enrolls in School of Engineering at Penn State College (PSC) (September)

1943   Enlists and enters World War II at Fort Belvoir's Engineering School
           (May 27)
       Begins instructing US Army recruits in engineering (November)

1944   Transferred overseas (December) to India, Burma, then China

1945   *World War II ends (September 2)*
       Reassigned to US Graves Registration in Shanghai as Sergeant Major
           (September)
       Works with Chinese Missionaries (desires to return to serve in China)

1946   Returns Home; Discharged from the Army (May 16) but remains in
           Reserves three years
       Returns to PSC as a Sophomore
       Joins Intervarsity Christian Fellowship; meets Jean Esbenshade and Don
           DeHart
       Begins teaching Chinese students' Bible study

1947   *Jean graduates*
       Pursues Jean in Lancaster; they begin dating
       Becomes engaged to marry Jean (December)

1948   Designs and helps build a new house for parents
       Marries Jean (June 5)
       Returns with Jean to State College to finish senior year at PSC

1949   Graduates in Engineering from Penn State University
       Gets part-time engineering job at Penn Boiler Company, Lancaster, PA
       Enrolls as Freshman at Lancaster School of the Bible (LSB)
       *People's Republic of China created – communism closes door to missionaries
           (October)*

1950   Starts the Missions Department at LSB; begins teaching missions courses
       Begins serving with Egypt General Mission (EGM), Treasurer

1952   Graduates with a 3-year degree in Bible from LSB
       Passes PA State Board Exam; becomes Licensed Professional Engineer
           (July)
       Leaves job at Penn Boiler
       Becomes industrial salesman for Richard's Photo Shop (November)
       Begins offering photo darkroom designs to Richard's customers

1954   Renovates Esbenshade Farmhouse for photo classes
       Esbenshade family gives land to LSB for new campus (April 4)
       Begins renovating additional existing buildings and developing LSB
           campus plan

1955   Moves into new home at 2072 Pine Drive
       Meets Oscar H. Hirt, Jr. at trade show in New York City

1956   Leaves Richard's Photo Shop
       Begins O.H. Hirt branch office and warehouse in Shillington, PA
       Begins designing and inventing darkroom equipment for customers

1957   Begins using PVC to create, produce and distribute Sebastian Darkroom
           Products

1958   Buys first Sebastian Miniature in Massachusetts and begins a collection

1960   *LSB relocates from Lancaster City to Esbenshade farm*

1961   Celebrates birth of daughter Nancy (September 17)
       Joins Calvary Church in Lancaster

1963   Completes first new building on campus: Esbenshade Hall dormitory

1964   Replaced by new Missions Director at LSB, concludes teaching
           (September)
       Becomes Unevangelized Fields Mission (UFM) board member when
           EGM merges with UFM/Crossworld
       Photography work becomes full time

1965   Joins LSB Corporation
       Becomes LSB Campus Development Engineer

1966   Joins Bible Club Movement (BCM) Board (serves through 2005, 39 years)
       Establishes Commercial Lab Service in Esbenshade basement

1971   *Death of Martin Esbenshade, Father-in-Law and O.H. Hirt Warehouse
           Manager*
       Moves the O.H. Hirt business from Shillington to Lancaster

1972   Receives US and Canadian Patents for Wash-Off Processor invention

1973   *LSB becomes Lancaster Bible College (LBC)*

1975   Becomes LBC Trustee

1976   Replaced again at LBC as Campus Development Engineer as others
           begin new building program

1979   *Nancy begins studying at LBC*
       President Peterson begins to make positive changes

1980   Reinstated as LBC Campus Engineer

1981 Accepts ownership of Lancaster branch from Oscar and renames
business HIRTECH
Attends first Sebastian Miniatures Convention in Massachusetts
Develops Sebastian Exchange Collectors Association

1984 *Daughter Nancy graduates from Lancaster Bible College*
Publishes first *Sebastian Miniature Value Guide*

1990 *Granddaughter Becky is born (November 17)*

1995 Transfers design skills from drawing board to the computer – learns
CAD (at age 72)

1998 Sells Commercial Photographic Service to Bob Wiker

2002 Sells HIRTECH to Dennis Fahnestock
Presents bronze bust of Founder and President Henry J. Heydt to LBC

2006 Sells Sebastian Darkroom Products to California Stainless Mfg., Inc.;
becomes consultant

2014 *Granddaughter Becky graduates from Lancaster Bible College*

2015 *Nephew Tim Grove dedicates his children's book,* First Flight Around the
World, *to Paul (who was born in the same year – 1924 – as that first flight)*

2017 Presents bronze bust of President Peter W. Teague to LBC
Publishes life story in *Son of a Blacksmith: Forging a Life of Faithfulness*

Appendix B

Ancestry

OF SPANISH DESCENT

The following account is an oral history passed on to me
by my parents and extended family.

In the late 1700s, the Sebastian Family lived in a castle with beautiful spacious grounds in eastern Spain. As Protestants, they were greatly persecuted by the Catholic Church who wanted their estate. Eventually forced to leave their home, they fled to Germany.

As time passed, the three sons married German girls and moved to Alsace-Lorraine, a small country between France and Germany which bordered the Rhine River in the Vosges Mountains. These enterprising young men soon learned about endless wealth and possibilities in a new country called America. They and their wives immediately set sail for the land of promise and good fortune. One couple headed to Chicago and another located in Pittsburgh. The final destination of the third brother is unknown.

Grandfather Sebastian

The Sebastians who went to the Pittsburgh area settled in Butler, Pennsylvania. They later resettled in nearby Zelienople, where they were blessed with a baby boy they named George Byards Bastian (my grandfather). I have not found documentation or anyone who can tell me how the name changed from Sebastian to Bastian.

According to the National Park Service's files on the Civil War, as well as the National Archives in Washington, George enlisted in the Union Army at age eighteen. He joined the 134th Pennsylvania Volunteer Infantry Regiment and saw action in several towns such as Sharpsburg, Maryland; Fredericksburg, Virginia; and Smithville, West Virginia; quickly reaching the rank of Sergeant. George's last assignment allowed him to serve as second lieutenant under General Joseph Hooker. In the Battle of First Wilderness near Fredericksburg, Virginia, a shell burst damaged his left foot. His wound prevented him from

These three pictures show George Byard Bastian, my grandfather, (left) in a tintype as a lieutenant in the Civil War infantry, (center) in a formal portrait taken in his 40s, and (right) painted after his death in 1907 by Sarah Speyerer, his sister and fine artist of porcelain.

further service, and he was honorably discharged with less than one year of total combat duty. It is recorded that the 134th Infantry Regiment lost five officers, and that 104 enlisted men were killed or mortally wounded. (I thank God He spared Grandpa.)

After the War, George married Caroline Endres and moved to Williamsport, Pennsylvania, where great prosperity came to them through the lumber industry. Four healthy children were born to George and Caroline Bastian: Frank, Josephine, Walter and James (my father). The day Dad was born in 1893, it is said that Frank rode his pony through the town calling to everyone, "I have a baby brother!"

Frank Bastian married Mary and they resided in Abingdon, Virginia. For many years Frank was Station Master for the Norfolk and Western Railroad Company in Abingdon, Virginia. Later, during his retirement, Frank visited Walter each summer. Frank and Mary never had children.

George and Caroline Bastian are posing with their daughter Josephine Canfield and the first of three sons who died one month apart from pneumonia. Later, her daughter Mary was born.

Josephine Bastian married Nathanial Canfield, a wealthy lumberman, and they lived at 304 Center Street in Williamsport. Their daughter, Mary, married Townsend VanGlahn and birthed Elsa. Aunt Jo and Uncle Nat also owned Riverton, a summer home along the Susquehanna River.

Walter worked as a civil engineer with the Reading Railroad in Philadelphia, where James later joined him. Of all of my relatives, I spent the most time with Uncle Walt and his wife Alta.

George Bastian operated a dry goods store on the square in Williamsport where customers bought wallpaper, yard goods, all

This old photo of Bastian's Pavilion shows Grandpa (in white vest) standing outside his store.

sorts of notions, and everything for holiday decorating. It was much like the five-and-ten-cent stores that became popular later on.

Williamsport was situated along the West Branch of the Susquehanna River which brought a deluge of flood waters each spring. Grandpa endured two major floods, but in the flood of 1889, he lost everything and suffered a great financial setback. He then ventured into a roofing business which he continued until his death in 1907. His relatively early death—compared to most of my family—was probably in large part due to his war injury and the stress of financial setbacks during the floods.

In this photo of Dad's boyhood home at 416 West 3rd Street in Williamsport, Walter stands by the bike at the far left, father George stands on the grass, mother Caroline stands on the porch, Josephine rides the trike in front of her, and Frank leans against the house.

Dad's Early Years

My father was born as James Endres Bastian in Williamsport in 1893. When Dad arrived, his youngest sibling, Walter, had already reached the age of 17. His mother was 45 and not pleased about having another baby. Sadly, he grew up as an unwanted child, left to his own devices. He loved nature and spent most of his time at his sister Jo's summer home on the Susquehanna River. He boated, fished and studied wild life. Jo cared a great deal for Dad and watched over him.

This is possibly the earliest photograph of my father, James Endres Sebastian, who at age 18 lived with his brother Walter at their estate, Neshaminy Hills; he is holding 4-month-old Walter Jr. who passed away shortly after this photo.

Dad didn't like school and dropped out in the fifth grade. Uncle Walter told Dad that if he wouldn't go to school, he should come to live with him and he'd get Dad a job on the Reading Railroad. He would have to change his name, though, to Sebastian, since Aunt Alta liked the original family name and they had gone back to it. The name change did not bother Dad, and working on the Reading Lines appealed to him.

A year later, at the age of 14, Dad lost his father and finally accepted his brother's offer of a home and job in Bucks County, just outside of Philadelphia. When Dad boarded the train in Williamsport, his best friend, Hugh Bubb, was the only one who came to see him off.

Uncle Walter's Family

Aunt Alta grew up in Virginia, where her father, the Reverend Dr. Cooper, pastored Richmond Baptist Church. The Coopers raised Alta to be a genteel lady in every possible way. She attended a girl's finishing school in Richmond where she learned the art of fine southern living, encompassing etiquette, entertaining, personal decorum and civility. Soon after she graduated, Dr. Cooper received a call to pastor the Baptist Church in Jenkintown, Pennsylvania, which brought Alta into Walter's acquaintance. They were married a short time thereafter.

Walter and Alta had only one child who lived past infancy, George Cooper Sebastian; he was seven years older than me. It was always my pleasure to spend time with him; he treated me like a favored younger brother. Each of my visits with him included show-and-tell with his latest projects and inventions.

When Dad lived in their home, Alta taught him etiquette and the finer points of life, such as social and table manners, the art of conversation, personal decorum and more. Years later, some of that rubbed off on me, I hope.

Walter got Dad a job as a lineman with the Reading Railroad. The heavy, outside work involved laying rails, climbing poles and stringing communication lines. Often a train derailment would call him out in the middle of the night to make repairs. At midnight one terribly stormy night, Dad climbed to the top of a pole to replace some wires. With lightning all around and in driving rain, his pole went down. He rode it to the ground, uninjured but badly shaken — and convinced he would look for different work.

Uncle Walter's home was a picturesque Bucks County farmhouse built in 1810. Among the rolling hills was a large meadow that bordered on the Neshaminy Creek in which George taught me to catch bass. I will always remember watching Uncle Walter working around the farm, busy in one place or another. There was always plenty to do on the farm.

My Maternal Coeyman Side of the Family

Uncle Walt's hired man, Harry Coeyman from nearby Hatboro, helped with the farm chores. Harry was a robust Scotchman, a pork butcher, a mechanic, and known as the champion wrestler of Hatboro. Every year in the town's Fourth of July parade, Harry would pull the Hatboro Fire Truck through the streets — using only a rope between his teeth.

Four children, Lizzie, Jennie, Lillie and Raymond, were born to Harry before his first wife died giving birth to daughter Mary (my mother). He then married Ellen, who unfortunately never cared very much for his children.

One day Harry brought his pretty 16-year-old daughter, Mary, to see the Sebastian farm. She had the day off from the Hatboro Plumbing Supply Company where she worked as the office manager. Mary and Dad met that day, and their romance commenced. Dad and Mom's love grew quickly, and they were engaged to be married early in 1914. On that day, Dad gave her a box of her favorite candy. Amidst the dark-chocolate-covered almonds, he had placed a beautiful diamond ring.

Mother wanted to work for a time before getting married, but Dad's wishes prevailed. On October 22, 1914, Dad (19) and Mom (17) were married in their first home in the Oak Lane section of Philadelphia. Those present were Grandpa and Grandma Coeyman,

Mary's (left) sisters were Lillian, Lizzie and Jennie.

This later photo captures Uncle Armon, Aunt Lillie and their son Junior.

Aunt Lillie and Uncle Armon Greul, and Uncle Walter and Aunt Alta Sebastian.

About a year later, they were blessed with their first child, Mary Josephine Sebastian, named in honor of my mother and Aunt Jo. Josie was gifted in music and at her high school graduation won the very first four-year music scholarship offered by Beaver College (now Arcadia College) in Jenkintown.

World War 1

When America entered World War I in 1917, Dad was initially exempt from serving in the military because he had to care for his family. Josie had turned three, and Mother was pregnant.

In 1918, Mom and Dad were blessed with a handsome baby boy, James Endres Sebastian, Jr, named to honor my dad. The couple rejoiced in their wonderful little family, a daughter and a son.

As the war persisted, the fighting required more and more men. Later that year, Dad was assigned to active duty. With many other young recruits, he boarded a train bound for a nearby army base on November 11, 1918.

Shortly after departure, Dad's train screeched to a halt in the middle of a field, tooting its whistle continuously. The town's fire sirens could be heard in the distance. Finally shouts reached Dad's compartment. "The Armistice is signed! The Armistice is signed!" Men jumped off the train and ran for their homes, Dad among them. I'm told it was a time of great rejoicing throughout the nation. And I praise God for saving my Dad and my family.

Armon is standing with my dad Jim (left), and (right) Frank, Dad and Walter are relaxing with my dog Troy and Frank's Boston Terrier, Mike.

Death and New Life

Just after the war, Josie and little James contracted influenza during the epidemic that swept the world and killed millions. My sister recovered in weakened health, but little James passed into the arms of Jesus in 1923 at the age of four. Mother and Dad were devastated.

God sent a messenger with help. Reverend Dr. Tupper, an itinerant preacher and osteopathic physician from Canada knocked at our front door. As he opened the Bible and read comforting words of God's grace, my parents learned of the marvelous provision of eternal life through Jesus Christ, God's Son. Almost immediately they both received Christ as their personal Savior.

This is one of the very few photos we have of James (sitting beside Josie).

My parents joined a Baptist church in nearby Southampton and became ardent Christians. They wanted to follow the Lord Jesus in every way possible, so they planned to be baptized at the upcoming Easter sunrise service. On that cold spring morning, the ice was broken on the churchyard pool, and they were immersed by Dr. Tupper. Year after year Dr. Tupper visited us, taught us God's Word, and treated our illnesses.

With the passing of my brother James, Mother and Dad asked the Lord for another son. The Lord gave them their second son on January 4, 1924, and they named me Paul Judson Sebastian. My middle name honors the ministry of Adoniram Judson, the first Baptist missionary to Burma. Interestingly, years later I would serve in World War II in India less than one mile from the Burmese border.

I thank the Lord for the heritage left to me by my ancestors.

My Namesake

Adoniram Judson, Jr. (1788-1850) ministered the Gospel to the people of Burma for almost 40 years, translated the entire Bible into the Burmese language, and impacted world missions through his faithful testimony.

Adoniram and Ann (known as "Nancy") Judson arrived in Calcutta on June 17, 1812. Both local and British authorities protested Americans evangelizing Hindus in the area, so the Judsons sought another mission field. They were ordered out of India by the British East India Company, to whom American missionaries were even less welcome than British (the United States had just declared war on England). Finally on July 13, 1813, they arrived in Burma, having been told that Buddhist Burma was impermeable to Christian evangelism. Judson already knew Latin,

Greek, and Hebrew. Together with his wife, they studied the language 12 hours a day with a tutor. It took three years to speak it, due to the radical structure difference between Burmese and Western languages.

Judson's first public meeting was held in 1819 and attended by 15 men, most of whom were just curious. Two months later, he baptized the first convert. There were 18 believers by 1822, and he had finished a grammar of the language (that is still used in Burma today) and a translation of the entire New Testament. He produced the first printed materials in the country, including 800 copies of his translation of the Gospel of Matthew.

This portrait of Adoniram Judson hangs inside Judson Baptist Church.
Photo Credit: Baptist Press

The Anglo-Burmese War (1824–1826) interrupted missionary work in the country. English-speaking Americans were easily confused with the enemy and thought to be spies. For 20 months, Judson was imprisoned, first at Ava and then at Aung Pinle, treated violently, tortured and starved. During that time, Ann suffered raging fevers, nursed an infant, and desperately tried to keep her husband alive and win his freedom. Shortly after he was released she and the child died.

The war brought much greater religious freedom to the Burmese people. Baptist membership doubled about every eight years for the 32 years between 1834 and 1866. Also after the war, Judson was pressed into service as a translator, first for the defeated Burmese, then for the treaty negotiations.

While fellow missionaries were going into the southern jungles, Judson shook off the depression that gripped him after his wife's death and set out on long canoe trips alone up the Salween River into the tiger-infested jungles to evangelize the northern people groups. In between trips, he pursued his lifelong goal of translating the entire Bible into Burmese. He began the translation in 1810; it was completed in 1834 and printed and published in 1835.

In April of 1835, he married a missionary widow, Sarah Boardman, and they had eight children (five survived into adulthood). She died on their way back to America ten years later. Judson continued the trip and enjoyed a tremendously successful tour of the eastern seaboard, raising missions awareness and funds needed for missionary activity.

On June 2, 1846, Judson married for the third time, to writer Emily Chubbuck, who he commissioned to write Sarah Boardman's memoir. They had a daughter born in 1847. Soon after her birth, Judson developed a lung disease. He passed away on April 12,

1850, and was buried at sea.

At the time of his death, Judson left a completely translated Bible, a Burmese-English dictionary still in use today, 100 churches, and over 8,000 believers. He even wrote two hymns: Our Father God Who Art in Heaven and Come Holy Spirit Dove Divine.

Each July, Baptist churches in Myanmar, Burma celebrate "Judson Day," commemorating his arrival as a missionary. Around the world, churches, colleges and buildings have been named in his honor. There is a feast day on April 12th in the liturgical calendar of the Episcopal Church (USA) to honor Judson. And during World War II, the United States liberty ship SS Adoniram Judson was named in his honor.

When I was named after Adoniram Judson, my parents had no way of knowing that at age 20, I would ride an elephant in Burma on a short leave from the army. I was stationed in Ledo, within walking distance of the Burmese border. They could also not have known that I would one day be on the board of a mission called BCM International, with an area director for the Myanmar, Burma region. Just today, as I was finishing the writing of this book, I received a letter from BCM explaining that this director has developed study notes and references to create the first Burmese Study Bible, providing a way for the 3 million Christians in Myanmar to better understand the Word of God for themselves. My parents did not know these things would happen, but God did.

Pray with me for Burma, where a meager 6% of the population is Christian. And praise the Lord for what He has done—and is doing—around the world for the glory of His Name!

Appendix C

Letters

From a box of over 300 letters sent and received during Paul's Penn State and war years, Nancy gleaned, excerpted and edited the most interesting missives to include in this appendix. The unedited, complete letters are on the book's website, (www.sonofablacksmith.com). These letters, in chronological order, are followed by a few words of commendation and appreciation sent to Paul after the war through the present.

Letters from College and the War

From Paul to the family

September 27, 1942 – Penn State, freshmen year

We had ROTC inspection Friday. The Cadet Lieutenant inspected all of us. Some of the fellows received demerits (which is one point off your final grade). He looked at me...my shoes were just shined before drill, and my sox are just the right shade (you saw them in my wash – 25¢ a pair) and I never need a shave (I only shave once a week) – my shoes are made of a very good leather and really shine. When he finished looking me over (I was standing at attention all this time—you can't even move a finger) he said "very good." I was the only one he said that to. If he said anything to you at all, he'd snarl, "Get a shave! Give him a demerit, Sargent!"

May 3, 1943 – Penn State

Today I read the official notice from the army about the ERC (my reserve). It stated ALL in the ERC would be notified at their homes after the close of this semester—May 12, 1943. Galbraith told me to get from my dean a sheet with questions which when I answer them will tell (pretty much) what I can do and my answers will help them place me in the army. I'm coming home Thursday evening, May 6 (late). One of my classmates is taking me to Reading in his car. From these I'll take the Reading R.R. home. Don't worry, Ma.

Official Postcard received at home from the War Department, Headquarters, Engineer Replacement Training Center, Fort Belvoir, Virginia

6-21-43 Pvt. Paul J. Sebastian is now: Company C, 5th Engineer Training Battalion, 4th Pn. Company Officer: W. J. Brown III, Lt. C.E.

July 26, 1943 – Fort Belvoir

Well, we slept late this morning – until 5:30 A.M. We studied and used all types of tools today. Air tools, gasoline chain saw, peavey axe, adze, pick, mall and all types of lumbering and carpenter tools. We ate chow from our mess kits at noon in the field. When we came back to camp this afternoon we got in khaki's (Army calls them "suntans") and had our platoon picture taken. Saturday at the shooting range I won 3 cigars and a pack of cigarettes (which I gave away). Tomorrow we have demolitions – that is, demolishing buildings, bridges, roads, tanks, etc. It should be very interesting. Pray for me.

July 29, 1943 – Fort Belvoir

We marched a good distance into the country today to study how to conceal trucks, bivouac areas, & machine gun turrets. I drank a quart of milk tonight and ate a pint of ice cream. I weigh 165, the same as I did when I entered the army.

Postmark: August 15, 1943, 8:30 P.M., Western Union Telegram

WM38, BV145 72 NL=BV FTBELVOIR VIR 14
MRS JAMES E SEBASTIAN=
15 CHEERY ST WILLOWGROVE PENN= = =:
I GOT MY NAME DOWN FOR A WEEKEND PASS. MOST LIKELY WILL GET IT IF EVERYTHING GOES ALLRIGHT. YOU CAN EXPECT ME FOR SATURDAY EVENING SUPPER AUGUST 20. THE DURATION OF THE PASS IS SATURDAY NOON TO MONDAY 6AM. HAVENT RECEIVED ANY MAIL FROM YOU IN 3 DAYS. GUESS ILL GET IT TOMORROW. LOVE= PAUL.

Letter from Uncle Frank Bastian, Langhorne, Pennsylvania

October 3, 1943

I do hope you will pass the examination as an instructor. It is worth trying because if you make the grade you will be entitled to additional passes to come home. Work hard! George was home last Sunday, September 26th, and of course we were all glad to see him. Hope he can come again next Sunday. He likes New York very much and says he can now find his way around in the subways.

From Paul to the family

January 10, 1944 – Fort Belvoir

There will be a lot of changes in the school in the very near future. I may be put on the availability list for overseas duty. Captain

Hammond jokingly asked me if I would like overseas combat duty. I told him I liked my nice set-up here, living so close to home. He said I wasn't on the list—yet. I think they will take the weakest instructors first for the overseas list. But unless I get a break, I don't feel too stable. I'm going to make application for a furlough

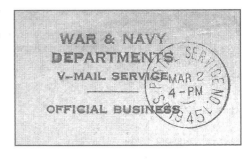

tomorrow—before it may be too late. I'm anxious to find out how Daddy's making out on the house, how Josie's voice is doing, and what Ma is cooking.

Letter from Dad

December 31, 1944

I took George to get his wisdom tooth taken out Christmas eve. The shock and pain of the abscessed tooth along with the strain he was under while he was in battle proved too much and he had to stay in bed

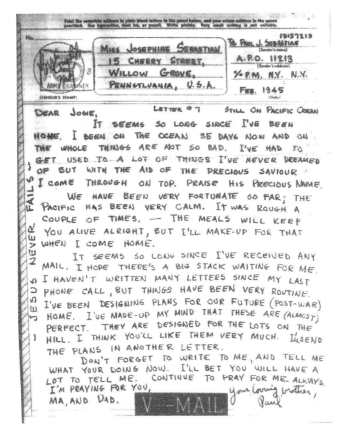

This 3"x4" V-Mail to Josie was written aboard ship.
(actual size)

Our letters were censored by an army superior (his name appears in the lower left corner of the envelope) who used a razor blade to cut out any sensitive information. Rarely were my letters cut, but here he removed the number of days we spent on the ship.

the day after Christmas. The next day, Uncle Walt and Aunt Alta drove him to Allentown for the plane back to his base. Son, we don't know where you are going, but no matter what happens to you, we want you back home just as soon as possible and no matter how severely you may be injured – we want you home with us. We are looking to the Lord Jesus to guide and protect you. By the way, I got my second check. That makes a full month at the new job, and I like it very much. I wish you a successful New Year, and the good Lord's blessings rest upon you throughout this year 1945.

From Paul to the family

February 23, 1945 – India (first letter sent after days of crossing the Pacific Ocean)

First, I want to say, I arrived safe and sound, although we came through some mighty dangerous waters. Praise the Lord for the safe journey. To go back to my letters that I wrote on the ship (#1-7), please take them with a grain of salt. I was under the first big change. It was as bad as I said, but I later adjusted myself as the trip went along... I passed time on the ship by working on our plans for our home which I will explain in a later letter. I'm enclosing a rough sketch of the house.

Well, I carved two notches in my Bible. I led two of my buddies to Christ. The first boy is Phillip Castro. The other is Bobby Meyer. The chaplain gave me four Gideon New Testaments (2 for spares) and a lot of tracts which I gave the fellows. They heartily accepted them and are reading. That was the greatest feeling of my life to lead those boys to Christ.

India is a land of romance and beauty, according to Kipling - but I

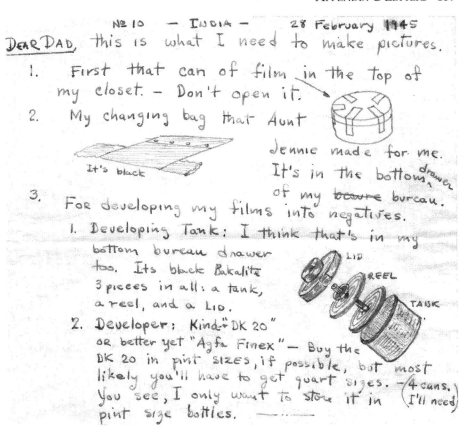

№ 10 — INDIA — 28 February 1945

DEAR DAD, this is what I need to make pictures.

1. First that can of film in the top of my closet. – Don't open it.

2. My changing bag that Aunt Jennie made for me. It's in the bottom drawer of my brown bureau.

It's black

3. For developing my films into negatives.

   1. Developing Tank: I think that's in my bottom bureau drawer too. Its black Bakalite 3 pieces in all; a tank, a reel, and a Lid.

   LID
   REEL
   TANK

   2. Developer: Kind "DK 20" or better yet "Agfa Finex" — Buy the DK 20 in pint sizes, if possible, but most likely you'll have to get quart sizes. (4 cans, I'll need) You see, I only want to store it in pint size bottles.

I couldn't wait to develop some of the incredible pictures I was taking in India, so I sent home a seven-page request for developing supplies, complete with diagrams (first partial page shown here).

don't think Kipling ever saw anything of India, because it's a land of filth and disease! Don't get worried, I'm so full of needle holes I whistle when the wind blows (that one really belongs to Bob Hope). But my most immediate danger is malaria. We have mosquito nets over our beds and a protective ointment for our skin. We live in 6-men tents, eat out of mess kits, and sleep on rope lattice beds with 3 GI blankets. It's very hot in the daytime and very cold at night. Our food is mostly canned but edible. I'm writing this by candle (one) light. Please send me white candles not taller than 6". It was really a rough hike from the train to camp in the heat, but the day was brought to a pleasant ending by our first mail call. I got 41 letters and 11 more today, making 52. What splendid letters. I'm still reading them.

Letters from Mother

August 4, 1945

Sunday dinner is over. Pa is taking a snooze and Josie has gone flying with Richard for the first time this summer. She looked OK in her brown slacks. A little on the stout side, but not bad at all. So I sat down to talk to my boy. Yesterday morning we received the large box of tea

This Nash-Lafayette automobile belonged to Dad during the Great Depression and throughout the war.

from you. I made iced tea for dinner today from our India Tea and we all thought it very delicious. I even gave a cup of it to Pal [Cocker Spaniel] so he could taste the tea his master sent. It surely will last a long time, there is so much of it – about 6 pounds. Pa gave the car a good bath and I cleaned all the smudges off the tapestry and windows.

I am dreaming of the wonderful Sebastian new home. I wonder when we can start building? Pa wants stone, but I'd rather have clapboard and have enough for the oil burner, 2 bathrooms and a nice kitchen.

Josie just finished giving us some piano music. She has an easy book for you to study when you come home—easy music, but effective and beautiful.

I have your picture where I can look at you all the time. It is so good, seems like you are right here. You are not too thin and not too fat—just right.

April 7, 1945

My pen just came back from Schaeffer Co. Iowa. It writes fine now, so I immediately started a letter to you. I didn't receive any mail from you yesterday or today. Maybe you are being transferred, or maybe it hasn't reached us. Or maybe you are letter-bound—have gotten so

Mother's letter penned April 7, 1945 was mailed to India in this envelope.

many letters all at one time you do not have them all finished reading?

Josie is having trouble with her singing voice which worries her, along with strain from taking over the new teaching job. She will soon have her permanent certification.

I was fortunate in getting a leg of lamb for this week, because as of April 1, new points are in use. I told Lillie and Armon they could stop in after church for dinner. Maybe Pa can get some help from Armon on your enlarger while we do the dishes.

I heard that Germany's war is all but over and will take a few weeks of cleaning up. And Japs will soon give up after that as their great fleet of ships is about gone. The Allies have complete control of the seas. I almost touched the ceiling with glee. I get every bit of news I can. Last Sunday I sat beside Mrs. Montage who says her boy is in the worst fighting. Mrs. Bessinger said her son was in the 3rd Army in Germany. And Mrs. Kirk says Ralph is in Germany too. Blanche's boys are in the service. Herbert was wounded in the shoulder, but he has just returned back to the service. The other boy, Harry, is in the Aleutian Islands.

I wore one of my butterflies to church yesterday. It sure was sweet of you to remember your ma with such a nice gift.

May 15, 1945

We received your letter all about the rainy season and the dampness and mold. I do not see how you are going to stand it for four months. I would think the boys would get pneumonia. I'm worried. I would suggest you wear a piece of newspaper or writing paper over your chest, holding it on with adhesive tape, to keep the dampness away from your lungs.

Monday morning, I mailed a box with your pajamas and a box with saltines, butterthins, a glass of peanut butter, a glass with a screwed top of apple jelly, a pkg. of marshmallows, a box of molasses candy kisses Josie bought at Strawbridge's and some other hard candy Pa brought home. I perspired tying them up Sunday evening. I tied and tied and tied. I sure hope it carries and that it will be intact.

It sure is good news if the Jap war will be over by October. That is the opinion of many. With the force of all our armies, we surely ought to lick them real quickly. I know how weary you are of being away. If it wasn't that we are planning for your coming home and what you and we are and expect to do, it would be terrible.

From Paul to the family

May 1945–Assam, India

I've almost completed the plans of our home. It's just within our means. I have the first floor and second floor plans completed (and furnished – just my suggestions, of course. Ma's will be better.) Let me describe it.

"Home Talk" As we walk in through the beautiful front door we see before us a lovely archway into the living room with an open staircase

On these stairs, my two-year-old Nancy is peeking through Dad's beautiful wrought iron railing—almost twenty years after I described my vision of the house-to-be-built.

and one of Dad's finest railings. Across the vestibule, with a small closet for guests' coats, we notice a pretty little dining room. We gaze upstairs and see a very interesting, spacious stairway with wide treads, and well-lighted by the living room and second floor hallway window.

...a two-way door leads into the perfect kitchen with no wasted space, and you don't have to walk a mile from the range to the sink to the refrigerator. Neatly worked in is a small breakfast nook with table and bench. Don't miss Ma's corner either, along with overhead cabinets and nice windows over the sink. Just inside the back door is a handy broom closet. Next to that is the door heading down to the basement, with a turn landing after two steps. *[ten additional pages continue this imaginative tour of the new house plans]*

May 11, 1945 – Assam, India

How's the sweetest Mother a fellow ever had? I always have your picture here in front of me, Ma – as I write to you. Once in a while I come in my darkroom during the day and say, "Hello, Mom." I write letters and read my Testament in my darkroom here – sort of my upper room, I guess.

Well, today was payday, and beer rations came out – so things are a little high around here tonight. It all seems so useless and false and such an ugly form of so called entertainment.

I've got things fixed up pretty good all around the tent here and everything's as homey and comfortable as possible. The chow is generally getting better, too. The water is doped-up pretty much with medicine – but one thing that can't be changed is its wetness – ha!

I've been studying a college catalog that one of the fellows has lent me. I studied in detail all the engineering courses (curriculums). Keep in mind: the government sends me free only if I can pass my subjects. I've got my eye on this Architectural Engineering Curriculum. I'd like to go an extra term to get a degree in Structural Engineering. I am anxious to hear what you and Dad and Josie and Dick have to say about it.

I hope the plans for the home have arrived by now. I am so anxious to know if anyone approves and if there are any additions or subtractions. I'm saving my money...

August 14, 1945 – Assam, India

Yesterday morning and this morning I blew reveille. It went off fine. My lip is weak, but it will become stronger in time. I get up at 5:45 and blow first call at 6:00, assembly at 6:10 and reveille at 6:15. Then chow, then work.

The Post Exchange opened an Indian Store with controlled prices. I bought some very nice pieces of brass and ivory that I know you'll love. I also sent home my Gurkha knife and that fan my bearer gave me. I had to saw the handle of the fan in half in order to fit it in the box. About that Japanese fan: the Vice-Commander presented it to me as a token of our friendship. He got it in Burma – took it from a Japanese soldier. He put a Chinese inscription on it which I will translate from memory when I get home. Take good care of it; I like it very much. All the brassware I have labeled Merry Christmas and to whom it is to go. I'll be home for next Christmas for sure.

Bob Koenig and I went up to teach the Chinese last evening. After the class, we returned to the commander's tent as is our custom and found some well-educated, high-ranking Chinese officers (majors and so on) who spoke fairly good English. We had a very enlightening talk along with the usual Chinese tea—such slurping you've never heard; Chinese table etiquette is far from what we consider polite. They asked us to take dinner with them at the Chinese restaurant in Ledo (it was 9 o'clock). After declining, we saw their regret and finally agreed, piling into two Jeeps and taking off. At the restaurant, they led the way past

This Gurkha knife I bought in Calcutta came in handy when a cobra slithered under the platform of my tent. (I stand at the far left; third is John Carr, from New York City, affectionately called "Pop" because he was drafted at age 39.)

the beggar's "boxeese sahib" and headed for the officers' entrance. I told the major that we couldn't go in as enlisted men, but he said that in the Chinese army there is no discrimination, and we were his guests. So, in we went and found a table—Bob and I and six Chinese officers. I happily put my arms on the table and displayed my stripes to the glaring American officers and the silly and giggling nurses.

The major scribbled down a lot of Chinese words to give to the Chinese waiter. Our plates were chinaware with handleless cups and china spoons, and chopsticks. Cold lime squash was served first, followed by the most delicious chicken broth, sauces, platters of roast chicken chopped into bite-size pieces, platters of liver and onions and cucumbers with a delicious gravy all over, platters of chopped pork with potatoes all smothered in gravy (most delicious) and big bowls of rice.

The Chinese officers ate right off the platters with their personal chopsticks – Josie would have been appalled. A couple of times, I couldn't raise my hand to eat – someone's arm was across my face, reaching with chopsticks for a tasty bite of chicken or something. The funniest thing was watching them eat a "cup" of rice, holding it to their mouth and "scooping" the rice in with their chopsticks – something like a conveyer belt.

Everything was extremely foreign in taste but delicious. We'll all have to have a meal or two in a Chinese restaurant when I come home. By the way, soup comes at the end of the meal; and tell Dick there's no dessert.

Everything's going as usual now, with plenty of rumors flying as to what will become of us here at Ledo. It's 11:30 PM now and at 12 midnight they are expecting to—I should say hoping to—announce the Japanese surrender over the radio.

V-J Day, 7 o'clock AM, August 15, 1945 – Assam, India

The official word of the Japanese surrender has been announced. The horns are blowing and the train whistles are blowing steam. The spirit of the fellows has jumped 100%. It seems like Christmas day around here, everyone so cheerful and thankful. Mac and I are going to a special chapel service tonight to thank the Lord for everything. Today was declared a holiday by General Yount. I intend to get caught up on my letter writing. I think (this is only my thinking now) that I'll be home sooner than I said in previous letters. As far as coming back to the "States" I don't think points will matter. But getting a discharge – points will count. When they stated the points (85) I had 27, so you see where I stand for discharge. If I have to serve some more time in the States, I'll ask to go back to Belvoir. The biggest thing (hindrance) in getting home will be the transportation problem.

August 30, 1945 – Assam, India

I got my orders yesterday for transfer to Chabua, to a Graves Registration outfit to care for our dead and their belongings. I'm pretty sure my work will be just paperwork, taking care of the card files, telling where, when, etc. about the burial of each man. I don't know how they picked me for the job, but I know that "He leadeth me" and that all of this is for a purpose. You remember me saying the situation here wasn't so good where I worked; well, maybe it's better where I'm moving. They say these Graves Registration outfits aren't very big – 4 men and an officer – so maybe I'll have a little more freedom.

Enclosed please find some Chinese money. Pop Car sent me some very nice pieces for my collections – also a Chinese water pipe. About my photo equipment. I'm taking my chemicals and developing tank with me so I can develop my film, and then I'll send the negatives home. How did you like the enlargements I sent home so far? I was quite pleased with them. I don't think I'll have any more time to enlarge after this.

Kodak's put out a camera called the "Metalist" that they have perfected; the Navy and Army have been using it about 18 months. I'd rather have it than my Leica because it takes a larger film, which doesn't have to be enlarged. Yep! Here I go buying another camera. This "Metalist" sells for $192.00 and my Leica costs $225.00, so I should be able to make an even swap.

Also, do you think I should get a car when I come home? It would be so handy to go to and from school. All my savings and war bonds should amount to $1000.00 which would pay for the car. Maybe a Chevrolet?

September 19, 1945 – Chabua, India

I'm glad they like Daddy down at the office. Did he get that raise?

This afternoon my orders came. We leave tomorrow or the next day for Shanghai. We fly the "Hump" (from Chabua to Kunming) in a C-46, a swell plane. Then we fly to Linchow and then to Shanghai. I hope they put us on a homeward bound ship when we hit Shanghai, but that's asking too much I guess (me with only 40 points).

The other day I received the nicest tin of cookies from Uncle Armon and Aunt Lillie. They were fresh as a daisy and delish. And

Uncle Armon and Aunt Lillie

yesterday I got that long-lost package of photo equipment (that was missing) and a nice box of salt water taffies from Dick.

November 27, 1945 – Shanghai, China (to Josie)

How's my sweet little sister? It's been nearly a year now since I've been home, hasn't it? Soon I hope to be homeward bound. Then I can start to live again, after three years of restrictions. I think I'll be able to make the grade scholastically and from the social aspect – I've seen so many people, lived with so many people, had so many forced upon me – it's been a real education alright...

I've been so busy these past days. I'm doing the jobs of about 3 or 4 men. The high point (70, 60, 55) men have left or are leaving and there are no replacements so I'm caught holding the bag. I sure wish I had a few more points.

Today I got my sweater, sox, handkerchiefs and peanut butter (all wrapped up in a Corset box – the fellows laughed!) Boy, this sweater was a welcome sight. It's getting pretty cold here now. I've been doing some shopping lately for you and Ma and Dad and Dick and others. I'll sure have a lot of fun unpacking my bag when I get home – we'll have a real Christmas. This letter should reach you just about 15 Dec, so a very Happy Birthday, Jo. I'll be home for all the rest.

December 22, 1945 – Shanghai, China

I'm writing this letter in the bed of the 172nd General Hospital with malaria. (Don't get worried now.) I guess one too many mosquitos bit me back in India. I'm feeling fine now, though, and the Doc says I can get out the day before Christmas. I felt it coming about two weeks ago. I was working my fool head off, I had a bad cold, and then one day we got in some heavy boxes of equipment and I sprained my back pretty

badly. That afternoon I started getting the chills. They're so bad you think you'll freeze to death. Then I'd get too warm in the evening and perspire. The next day, with a temperature of 102.6°, I was sent to the hospital where it increased to 104.4°. They did blood tests, and then the nurse told me I had malaria and started me on a month of Adabrin treatment. She also gave me something

When Ma received the letter about the malaria and hospital stay, she drew this picture of his beloved pet and sent it to her boy.

to make me sweat it out, and man, did I sweat! But I slept pretty good that night and felt much better in the morning. The good news is I'd have to get bitten by another malaria mosquito before I'd get this strain of malaria again. I've sure had a lot of visitors.

Just days to Christmas and it sure looks like it's going to snow...

Letter from Sister Josie

March 17, 1946

Thinking of you and wondering how near you are to coming home! We have not heard from you for several weeks now but hope to hear some good tidings very soon. Every day is the same for me, working hard at my job and waiting, like all the rest of the family, patiently for your home coming.

I got a beautiful new straw spring hat to come meet you on your homecoming. I am all set to go sporting with you when you come home...

Ralph Kirk is home and is discharged. How happy the Kirks are! Ralph looks O.K. no outward physical defects. Just lost some of his hair from wearing a helmet all the time.

Letter from Mother

March 19, 1946

We're so happy to be able to count on your homecoming in April!

Pa thinks maybe you should join the reserves, in order to keep your rating. There is an active reserve and an inactive reserve, from what we gather. The active reserve has to train for a couple of weeks each summer. You don't have to do anything for the inactive reserve, and after 5 years you are automatically dropped from the roll. Many people are saying we will probably have a war with Russia within five years. One man on the radio said we won't have any more wars because our atomic bomb will end anything before it starts. I don't know what to advise. I just want you to be free and happy.

From Paul to the family

April 17, 1947 – Post-War letter from Penn State

I've been thinking about this summer and asking the Lord about a job for this summer.

I told Mrs. McCormick to reserve her spare room for you on June 6. Ma and Jo can sleep there and Dad with me.

Sunday I speak at the prison 9:30 AM. Be much in prayer that He might give me great power to tell of the Love of God. The Lord has laid verses upon my heart – oh, that I might do justice to these great words by His Spirit. "Not I, but Christ."

Over my radio yesterday came the nation-quaking awful news of Texas City...a great disaster! Immediately I thought: that awful, awful condition is just a little bit of what hell is going to be like. Then as I came home from supper after the rain, I looked into the heavens and saw the sun's rays beautifully piercing the broken clouds. I immediately thought: that beautiful sight is just a little bit of what the Great Day when Jesus will come for us will be like.

These letters from Mother, Father and Josie all arrived in the same envelope, written on October 5, 1947. Note that Mother and Josie both refer to Jean as if she and Paul are already engaged, which is not official until mid-December.

October 5, 1947

Mother – We are more than homesick for our boy, especially me. I miss you more each day. It is wonderful how you applied yourself away from home and won the respect of everyone. I surely am proud of you. We will pray for you as you speak at the prison.

You worked so hard this summer on our new home, and I sincerely pray you will have a nice term. It will go better knowing you have a dear sweet girl you are engaged to. I know how happy Jean is too. She seems sensible and I know will make you a good wife. She isn't like the general run of girls today. Glad she has such a good job and so near at home...

Dad – The report of the builder to the architect goes like this:

All dozen windows are in and centered

All 2nd floor joists are in place

Bridging is ¾ way along on the joists over the living room only...

I got all the lumber but the oak and maple flooring...

Received all the paint for outside and inside...

Bought a new 24' ladder and a new 6' step ladder

Josie – It isn't the same around here since you left to go back to college. I have gone up to our new home sometimes in the evenings to help Pa. I enjoyed it except I missed my young good-looking boss. Everybody wants to know where the young boss is, then Pa gives a deep sigh and tells how hard it is without you, honey. Glad you and my new sister are making out so fine. I surely do like her. Hope she will like me as much.

From Paul to the family

October 30, 1947 – Penn State

I am so happy that everything is going just fine for you and the home. The Lord will surely send someone with $8500.00 for the [Cherry Street] house. Thanks for getting me the money [for Jean's engagement ring]... It's really a beauty, all for my Jeanne – oh how I love her and oh how she loves me and oh how we love and thank the Lord for our parents and dear sweet sisters...

A note sent from Penn State about two months after the wedding – from Paul, Jean and Jean's sister, Kathryn, who is visiting

August 3, 1948

Paul – How I praise God for my lovely wife – she's so sweet in every way. Don was up for the IVCF conference this past weekend. Mr. Heydt was our guest speaker, and I was conference leader and enjoyed my job so much. The Heydt's brought Kathryn up for the conference and to stay a week with us. When can Josie come up? I have more than a dozen sermons in mind for the August 11th service at the prison.

Thanks manifold times for your prayer for us and for Aug 11 too.

Jean – Thanks so much for the birthday card and the $3.00 gift. It was so sweet of you to remember me and I wanted to thank you sooner but we were so rushed over the weekend. Friday evening, after Bible Fellowship meeting, Miriam Krebs, my girlfriend up here you know, had a birthday surprise party for me – a real surprise! Thanks again for the gift!

Kathy - How are you getting along with your hard school work in the hot summertime? It surely won't be long before mine starts again. I'm having a real nice time on a few vacations now before it starts. oxoxox

Army Commendations

The following three letters of recommendation were written by Paul's commanding officers in 1944 on stationary from Headquarters: The Engineer School Department of Mechanical and Technical Instruction Fort Belvoir, Virginia

From John W. Steinmann, 2nd Lt. C.E.

...Based on his record here I can recommend Paul without any reservations. He has proved himself to be most industrious and cooperative and very thorough in his approach and solutions to any problem he had had to solve...

From William Hammond, Capt. Corps of Engineers

Tec. 4 Paul J. Sebastian finished first in his class with a superior rating, and was retained as an instructor in the course. He was enthusiastic and industrious as an instructor, and at the same time he was a squad leader in his company. Sebastian did a good job on every assignment, which sometimes went far beyond normal duties. He is a qualified draftsman, construction foreman and photographer.

From R.W. Watt, Major, C.E., Supervisor, Topographic Section

...Sebastian has displayed keen intelligence, initiative, and an inexhaustible capacity for work. He has conceived, designed and constructed many of the training aids used in our drafting courses and had contributed materially to the construction of a completely modern map-reading classroom. Sgt. Sebastian can follow an assignment through to its completion in an efficient manner with a minimum of supervision...in the areas of surveying, carpentry, electrician, photographer, machinist, blacksmith, welder, and construction foreman. He is an undergraduate engineer and has a well-rounded background as a mechanical, architectural and topographic draftsman.

Letters of Appreciation

These last letters express recognition and appreciation for Paul's character and service.

From Don and Vicki, a couple Paul photographed on their wedding day

Dear Mr. Sebastian,

You, your lovely wife and Nancy have been so very kind to us. You very evidently live out your lives with Christ in the forefront. You have played such a big role in this precious event in our lives. You are a topnotch person—and photographer. Thanks for making us the happy exception to your retirement from weddings.

From Eric G. Crichton, Pastor, Calvary Independent Church

January 1977

On behalf of the Official Board and the entire congregation let me assure you of our deepest gratitude for your faithful service as a deacon and as a member of the Official Board...and for the outstanding contribution which you made to our building program in serving as architect. We are very grateful for your generosity and also for the excellent design of our new facility...

From Charles E. Piepgrass, Th.D., Associate Director, Unevangelized Fields Mission (UFM)

July 1978

Thank you again for sharing with our candidates in the area of photography, instructing them in techniques, and offering them equipment options that would be useful in their missionary service. This is a very practical contribution to their month and we are grateful for your willingness to do this...

From Alfred Larson, General Director, UFM

November 1978

So many folks have spoken to us about the tremendous blessing they received from the banquet and over and over again they mention how tremendous the slide presentation was. Paul, you did such a super job on the preparation of the slide-tape presentation. We realize you not only spent a good amount of time in preparation, but also invested financially in making the presentation the excellent one which it was...

From Joe Rowe (employed as the company's service manager)

The generous bonus came very unexpectedly. It was a pleasant surprise. I also want to thank you for the recent raise in pay. I value the opportunity to work for you and Oscar Hirt Inc.

From a young LBC student who served with Paul in the Audio Control Room at Calvary Church

I count it an honor to call you friend and even in some ways look to you as a father. During the coming school year, I hope to spend a Sunday a month in the control room and hope that we might be able to share that service together. If I can also be of any help to you in your basement studio ministry let me know, as I would sincerely like an opportunity to work with or for you...

Compilation of excerpts from letters by LBC President and dear friend Gil Peterson from 1980-1984

Paul, you frankly overwhelm me with your thoughtfulness and enthusiasm for this vital ministry. The excellent manner in which you have served as Secretary of the Board has been appreciated greatly by each member, and your reelection to this position is evidence of the confidence that they have in your ability. Thank you also for your labor in such areas as the revised site plan, pictures, and using your talents in so many different ways. Your sacrificial giving of yourself, time and financial support is so deeply appreciated.

Your gracious manner and willingness to do tedious and repetitive things with joy and satisfaction really makes the difference in the operation of the board and its committees. I count you as a dear friend and love Jean for the way she supports your work in ministry...

Gilbert A. Peterson, President
Lancaster Bible College

Appendix D

Recipes

Aunt Alta's Gee Whiz Cake

Yummy! – mentioned at the end of Chapter 2

Preheat oven to 350°F.

Ingredients:
    1 cup sugar
    1/2 cup lard (or 1/3 cup butter, margarine or solid shortening)
    1 cup water
    1 cup raisins (large Muscat raisins were Aunt Alta's favorite)
    1 1/2 cup flour
    1/4 teaspoon each – ginger, nutmeg, cloves and cinnamon
    1 teaspoon baking soda
    1/2 cup walnut pieces
    1/4 cup brown sugar

Directions:
Boil sugar, lard, water and raisins in a quart pot on medium high heat until mixture comes to a boil (stir often). While this is cooking, combine the flour, spices and baking soda in a medium-size mixing bowl. Add the hot raisin liquid (reserve the raisins) to the dry mixture and mix thoroughly. Add the raisins and walnut pieces. Pour into a greased one-layer cake pan or 8"x8" pan and top with brown sugar. Bake at 350°F for 45 minutes, until a toothpick poked in the center comes out clean.

Yields about 8 servings.

Brubaker Family Cracker Pudding

Mentioned in the story about the Brubaker Christmas Dinner, Chapter 8

Preheat oven to 425°F.

Ingredients:
  2 cups milk
  1 egg (separated)
  1/2 and 1/4 cup sugar
  1/2 cup crumbled saltines crackers
  1/3+ cup coconut
  1/2 teaspoon vanilla extract

Directions:
Scald milk in saucepan; add egg yolk, 1/2 cup of sugar, cracker crumbs and coconut. Mix well, stirring until thickened. Remove from heat and stir in vanilla. Pour in baking dish.
Beat egg white until stiff and add sugar to make meringue. Spread over pudding and bake at 425°F for 5 minutes.

Yields 4-5 servings.

Mother Esbenshade's Baked Corn

Nancy and Tim really love this holiday side dish their grandmother always made with homegrown corn she cut off the cob and froze during harvest.

Preheat oven to 350°F.

Ingredients:
> 2 cups homegrown corn cut off the cob (if frozen, thaw first)
> 2 beaten eggs
> 1 cup milk
> 1 tablespoon sugar
> 1 1/2 tablespoons flour
> 1 teaspoon salt
> 1/8 teaspoon pepper
> 2 1/2 tablespoons melted butter
> 1/2 crushed cracker crumbs (saltine or other plain crackers)

Topping: 1/3 cup crushed cracker crumbs and 2 tablespoons butter

Directions:
Drain corn and stir together with other ingredients. Put in greased 1 1/2 quart baking dish. Stir together topping ingredients and add to tip of casserole. Bake at 350°F for 35 minutes (uncovered). Check to see if done by inserting a knife or toothpick that comes out clean.

Yields 4-6 servings.

Cranberry Raspberry Jell-O Salad

Jean's delicious meals are often enhanced by this delicious Jell-O salad, a regularly-requested holiday treat.

Cranberry Relish

Ingredients:
- 2 12-ounce packs of fresh cranberries
- 1 large unpeeled orange
- 1 medium unpeeled apple (Gala recommended)
- 1 1/2 cup sugar
- 2-3 drops of red food coloring

Directions:
Finely grind the three fruit in a food processor. Add the sugar and food coloring (optional) and stir. (Can be made ahead and refrigerated or frozen.)

Yields approximately 2 quarts.

Jell-O Salad

Ingredients:
- 1 3-oz. pack of dark cherry Jell-O
- 1 3-oz. pack of raspberry Jell-O
- 1-2 cans Oregon seeded dark (Bing) cherries (drained)
- 1-2 medium cans fruit cocktail (drained)
- 1 1/2 cups cranberry relish (see recipe above)
- 1 cup chopped nuts (walnuts recommended)

Directions:
Make Jell-O according to the directions on the packaging. Cool in the refrigerator until slightly thick. Then add the remaining ingredients, stir and refrigerate. Serve with whipped topping.

Yields 10-12 servings.

Jean's Quickie Chocolate Cake

An easy-to-whip-up staple or quick treat for unexpected company

Preheat oven to 350°F.

Ingredients:
- 1/2 cup vegetable oil
- 1 egg
- 1 cup sugar
- 1 1/4 cup flour
- 3 tablespoons cocoa (powder)
- 1/2 teaspoon baking soda
- 1/2 teaspoon salt
- 1/2 teaspoon vanilla extract
- 3/4 cup water
- 1/2 cup chocolate chips (optional)
- 1/2 cup nuts (optional)

Directions:
Completely combine all ingredients (in a bowl or directly in your 8"x8" baking pan). Cover with chocolate chips (and nuts, if desired). Bake at 350°F for 35 minutes, until a toothpick poked in the center comes out clean. Serve warm or cool; no icing needed.

Yields 9 generous servings.

Questions for Reflection or Discussion

1. How were Paul's recollections of the Great Depression different or similar from other accounts you have read or stories you have heard from people who lived then?

2. Paul mentions several teachers who had both positive and negative impact on his life. Which of your teachers do you most clearly remember, and why?

3. In chapter 2, Paul recounts his journey to accepting Jesus as his Savior. What is your story?

4. Time and time again, his life plan shifts and God leads him along: to college, to war, to prepare for the mission field, and then to stay home and help others become missionaries. How has God changed your plans over the years and led you in His ways?

5. Throughout the book, an array of friendships are mentioned: childhood neighbor friends, college buddies, etc. Look back at your life and consider who have been your friends, why, and what they've added to your life.

6. Twice at LBC, Paul was "fired" or displaced (as a teacher and as an architect). How did he handle those two difficult times? What kinds of disappointments have you experienced, and how have you worked through them?

7. As you read about Paul's 80-year photography hobby/career, what aspects of picture-taking were familiar and what was something intriguing you didn't know before?

8. Two sub-themes in the book are food and family. Take one or both areas and think about how they impact your life. Are you a foodie? And how has your family impacted your life for good?

9. At the end, Paul lists his "Holy Moments." What are some "Holy Moments" in your life?

10. Do you agree with the 11 life lessons Paul submits? Which ones have you already learned and regularly practice? Which ones would you like to work on? What else would you add?

11. Of the verses he lists in his concluding thoughts, which one(s) is your favorite, and why/how is it meaningful to you?

12. In Nancy's afterword, she mentions several things about her dad that impacted her. Choose a parent, teacher or mentor for your life and describe how they positively touched your life.